For the Shattered Soul

Catharine LJ Parks

Published by Catharine LJ Parks, 2017.

While every precaution has been taken in the preparation of this book, the publisher assumes no responsibility for errors or omissions, or for damages resulting from the use of the information contained herein.

FOR THE SHATTERED SOUL

First edition. January 2, 2017.

Copyright © 2017 Catharine LJ Parks.

ISBN: 979-8224361335

Written by Catharine LJ Parks.

Also by Catharine LJ Parks

Obese People

Obesity Strongholds: How to Overcome Them

Standalone

For the Shattered Soul

The Ins and Outs of Gastric Bypass

Tips For Successful Dining Out

I am a Keto Kid

Why Remain Morbidly Obese

Ten Fads to Stay Clear of

Don't let Fear Win

Arguing With God

Heaven Sent Signs and Wonders

Watch for more at www.catharineljparks.com.

Table of Contents

DEDICATION

To my Lord and Savior who has redeemed me by His blood. This book is dedicated to all the people who are trying to deal with the pain within. May God heal your soul and make you whole.

Table of Contents

CHAPTER 9
ARE YOU SLY?

CHAPTER 13
THE NATURE OF RAGE

The ancient Greek myth of the Furies and the writings of Roman philosopher Seneca highlight the dangers of unchecked rage. The Furies tormented those who committed great wrongs, while Seneca warned that "He who does not restrain his anger will be restrained by it." These lessons underscore the importance of managing anger before it consumes us.

Rage obscures our connection with God, creating a barrier between us and His love. True repentance involves seeking His guidance to overcome anger and restore relationships. By focusing on God's love and seeking His forgiveness, we can break the cycle of rage and embrace healing.

CHAPTER 14
THE FRAGMENTED SOUL

For those who genuinely desire to invite Jesus into their lives as their personal Savior, a sincere and heartfelt prayer of repentance and faith marks a crucial initial step in their spiritual journey. This prayer serves as a powerful expression of commitment, signaling a willingness to trust in Jesus for eternal salvation and redemption.

CHAPTER 1
INTRODUCTION FOR THE SHATTERED SOUL

Imagine carrying the weight of your past every day, like a heavy burden that refuses to lift. Many of us live in this reality, haunted by the ghosts of our past. Memories of hurt, betrayal, and trauma linger, affecting our daily lives and relationships.

For the Shattered Soul gives hope to those trapped by a painful past. This book guides you to heal your soul. It will help you mend deep wounds that have left you feeling used, abused, empty, and trampled on.

Think of the Phoenix rising from the ashes, strong and resilient. That's what this book aims to help you achieve. By facing and overcoming your issues, you can emerge stronger.

For the Shattered Soul uses real examples and powerful stories. They show you that you are not alone in your pain. Others have walked this path and emerged victorious, and you can too.

This book won't erase your past. But it will give you the courage, resilience, and strategies to heal and move on. It's time to let go of the emotional baggage that's been weighing you down and start living the life you deserve.

I will guide and support you on your journey of self-discovery and healing. I will help you heal your fragmented soul. I'll use counselling and spiritual direction.

For the Shattered Soul is more than a book. It's a roadmap to spiritual wholeness. It shows the path God has for you. It's an invitation to rediscover your true self. Be free from the shame, guilt, and fear that have held you captive for so long.

God's prophecies are not just words on a page. They are life-changing promises of hope, comfort, and encouragement. I share these sacred messages with those who will listen. They must use them in their lives and their loved ones' lives. As you read, I pray you'll find the courage to face your brokenness. Trust in God's power to restore you to wholeness.

As a student in the class of life, I've learned to ask for healing, forgiveness, and restoration. I've applied these lessons to unresolved issues that have held me back from fully enjoying life.

Through my struggles, I've discovered the keys to unlocking inner peace. I've learned to let go of the past and find freedom from emotional pain. Now, I share these keys with you. They will help you find your way out of darkness into the light of spiritual wholeness.

My personal, intimate moments with the Lord have taught me. I now know the depths of His love and concern for us.

As His beloved offspring, we are precious to Him, just as our children are precious to us. Our Heavenly Father's love is infinitely greater, for we are the fruit of His divine labour, created in His image.

This book will guide you on a journey of surrender. It will teach you to give up on human understanding. Instead, lean on the Lord's infinite wisdom and guidance. You will learn to trust in His sovereignty, even when the path ahead is uncertain. You will find peace in surrendering your life to His loving care.

Its pages will give you insight into your life. The Lord will nudge you toward the right path. This awareness will ready your heart, mind, and spirit to receive the healing you seek.

The life-changing principles within this book have the power to revolutionize your existence. They will free you from past heartaches and current troubles. You'll escape the shackles of emotional pain. This journey will transform you. The weights that dragged you down will be replaced by peace, joy, and love.

These pages hold wisdom. Use it to heal your life. Look within yourself. You will find peace, joy, and love will grow as you seek enlightenment. This journey of self-discovery will light the dark. It will guide you to a brighter future. There, you will find solace, comfort, and peace.

Why continue to carry the burden of emotional scars that only bring more pain and heartache in the days to come? Imagine breaking free from the past. Regrets and challenges have held you back for too long.

Now, you stand at the edge of a new beginning. The journey ahead will reveal hidden strengths within you. You'll learn to forgive and let go of the past. This freedom will give you a sense of newfound power. You'll start to see the world with fresh eyes, full of possibilities and promise.

Now, step forward into this new life. You'll find a sense of calm in your daily routine. Fear and anxiety will fade away. You'll start to see yourself in a new light, as a strong and capable person.

Take the first step toward freedom from emotional pain. Open your heart and mind to new ideas. Let go of past hurts and worries about the future. Focus on the present moment. This is where healing begins.

Start this new chapter with confidence. You've made the brave decision to let go of the past. Now, it's time to build a life that brings you joy. Every step you take will lead you closer to happiness. You'll discover a sense of purpose, and your heart will fill with hope and excitement.

Embrace this new chapter with courage. You'll find people who support and care for you. They'll help you stay on track and celebrate your successes. You'll learn to love and accept yourself, just as you are. This self-love will bring you peace and happiness.

This book presents a unique opportunity to rewrite the narrative of your life. Trade the pain and heartache for a healing glow. Let it lift the burden of your past wounds. Finally, peace and wholeness are within reach. This book will help you.

It will turn your darkest chapters into a story of resilience, hope, and triumph. It will light your way forward with a new sense of purpose and belonging.

Learn God's purpose for your life—let Him heal you in the areas where life has held you back. Don't miss out on opportunities in life because of your past.

Imagine waking up each morning with a sense of freedom and hope. The weight of past mistakes and current struggles no longer holds you back. You're no longer trapped in a cycle of pain and regret. Instead, you're moving forward with confidence and purpose. This is the life God desires for you—a life where your past no longer defines you but fuels your growth and success.

Be the person who fulfills their life's mission because you sought help. It's time for bold action. Like Nelson Mandela, who spent 27 years in prison, then led his country to democracy. He did this by seeking guidance from peers and mentors. He applied their life lessons to his heart.

Asking for help shows strength, not weakness. It shows your drive to reach your goals. Imagine the courage to admit you need support. Like a sailor in treacherous waters, you would rely on a trusty compass to find a safe harbour.

Act now—apply these words of encouragement to your heart. This is your chance to change your life. Like a caterpillar that becomes a butterfly after waiting for the right moment. The time is now; don't let fear hold you back.

Don't let fear whisper "you can't" in your ear. You can overcome any obstacle when you seek help. Look at J.K. Rowling, who went from being a single mom on welfare to a bestselling author. She didn't let her struggles define her. Instead, she poured her heart into her writing, and it paid off.

Embrace your new path with confidence. You've taken the first step by asking for help. Now, believe in yourself. Trust that you have the power to overcome any challenge. Remember, every great achievement starts with a single step.

You've shown great bravery by seeking help. It's a key step in overcoming the hurdles that have held you back. This brave act can spark positive change. Now, focus your energy on setting clear, achievable goals that align with your vision.

To achieve your goals, divide them into manageable tasks. This approach has helped diverse individuals, including entrepreneurs, athletes, and artists. For instance, when NASA planned to send humans to the moon, they broke the huge project into smaller tasks.

These included designing the spacecraft, testing the rockets, and training the astronauts. By doing so, they made the impossible seem possible.

Dividing goals into small tasks makes them seem more achievable. Imagine trying to climb a massive mountain all at once versus taking it one step at a time. This strategy lets you focus your energy on one task. It makes progress feel more tangible.

As you complete each task, you'll build momentum. It will be like a snowball rolling, gaining speed and size. Soon, you'll make steady progress toward your goal. That sense of accomplishment will propel you forward.

Olympic athletes often focus on small, incremental goals in training. They avoid letting the ultimate prize overwhelm them. Entrepreneurs divide their business plans into manageable tasks, clarifying the path forward. This approach will help you celebrate your progress. It will keep you motivated and help you reach your vision.

As you reach each milestone, celebrate your wins. They may seem small, but they matter. These small achievements are vital. They are the building blocks of your self-assurance. With each success, your confidence will grow. It will be like a muscle that gets stronger with regular exercise and commitment.

Imagine a weightlifter. They start with a lightweight barbell. They hoist it overhead with ease. They increase the load in small increments. This tests their endurance and pushes their muscles to adapt. With each successful lift, their strength grows. They can now tackle heavier loads with ease.

This growth in confidence will help you stay committed to your goal. You will face setbacks, but don't let them discourage you. Every athlete, entrepreneur, and weightlifter faces obstacles. They don't give up. Instead, they learn from their mistakes and move forward. You can do the same.

You end self-doubt by completing tasks, no matter their size. The more you achieve, the more your confidence grows. It's like a weightlifter's muscles. As you use your confidence, it grows. It empowers you to tackle tougher tasks.

For instance, imagine finishing a tough work project. You get great feedback from your colleagues. This success gives you the confidence to take on an even more demanding project, and so on. Each success builds your confidence, like a weightlifter's strength. It will help you tackle tasks that once seemed impossible.

CHAPTER 2
WORD OF ENCOURAGEMENT

God's whisper echoes within, urging us to share all with Him. This whisper is an open invitation to surrender our lives, desires, and our will to His greater plan. It's a call to obedience, to put His interests above our own, and to be willing to make sacrifices for the sake of others.

In responding to this invite, we'll change. We'll find new purpose and meaning in our lives. As His children heal, break free, and empower themselves, we will see miracles. They will reflect God's character.

God, our compassionate Father, wants us to know. He has seen our heartaches, wiped away our tears, and heard our desperate pleas. He chooses and qualifies those He has called, yet many of us run from our gifts instead of embracing them.

You may feel the need to prepare or refine your skills but rest assured—God knows exactly what He's doing. He is the master craftsman, shaping and moulding you for greatness.

All you need is a willing heart. He murmurs in your ear, so give a swift reply. Be faithful to small things. He will then trust you with greater tasks. He will unlock the floodgates of Heaven, pouring out His blessings upon you in abundance.

Now, be brave and take that first step. God's power will begin to flow through you like a river, washing away your fears and doubts.

As you obey Him, you'll see His divine plan unfold before your eyes, exceeding your wildest dreams.

Your life will become a powerful witness, drawing others to His loving heart. The more you yield to His guidance, the more He'll reveal His glory through you.

Don't let Satan, the sly and cunning enemy, rob you of your precious peace. The Lord bestowed His flawless, steady peace upon us as a gift.

Focus on Jesus, the source and perfecter of your faith, who masterminds every aspect of your life. He has everything under His control, like a master conductor. He guides each musician in an orchestra to play in harmony. This sovereign control brings comfort, as it did for the apostle Paul when he wrote to the Romans,

"And we know that in all things God works for the good of those who love him, who have been called according to his purpose" (Romans 8:28).

By trusting in God's sovereignty, you can rest assured that He is working everything out for your good, even amid the turmoil.

For the battle-hardened veteran of faith, the time has come. It is time to abandon the simplistic nourishment of spiritual infancy. They must now indulge in the robust, life-giving sustenance of God's sacred scriptures.

We must delve deeper. We must examine and ponder His divine revelations. They hold profound wisdom. As we explore God's Word, He will unveil kingdom mysteries. He will reveal hidden truths to those who, with devotion, seek Him and crave spiritual growth.

The scriptures, written by inspired authors thousands of years ago, hide ancient secrets. They have been unknown to humans for centuries. These mysterious truths, like hidden treasures, await the fervent. They seek a deeper understanding of God's divine nature. The scriptures are a rich tapestry of history, prophecy, and wisdom. They whisper hints of their secrets to those who listen with an open heart and a curious mind.

Like an archaeologist brushing away dirt to uncover an ancient city, a diligent student of scripture digs for hidden meanings in the text. Each discovery, like an artifact unearthed from the sands of time, reveals a fresh facet of God's multifaceted character.

As scripture's mysteries unfold, the seeker's understanding of God deepens. It is like uncovering a masterpiece painting, layer by layer until the full majesty is revealed.

They begin to comprehend the vastness of His power, much like the Amazon River, which carves out canyons and reshapes the landscape over time. Just as the river's current wears down the hardest rock, His love flows with an unstoppable force. It envelops everyone it touches, smoothing humanity's rough edges.

His wisdom is a beacon of hope that pierces through life's darkest moments, illuminating a path forward. Like a sturdy lighthouse, it stands tall against raging storms. It offers security and direction to those navigating life's turbulent waters.

Its guidance is a reassuring presence. It leads souls through the blackest nights to the promise of eternal life. In this sacred realm, weary travellers find hidden treasures and riches. They also find unexpected blessings.

It's like a master cartographer uncovering a long-lost treasure map. These treasures, forged in the depths of his wisdom, glow warmly. They remind us that, even in the darkest times, there is always a way forward.

We've all faced dark moments when the path ahead seemed uncertain and the world around us was in turmoil. At times, we've faltered, our feet slipping on the slick rocks of uncertainty, or wandering off course, lost in the dense fog of fear and self-doubt.

Yet, despite our doubts, we have reached out for the Savior's hand. At times, it was a blind hope. But He has been there, a steady anchor in the storm, guiding us through life's treacherous waters.

Like a lifeline, He's kept us afloat. He's saved us from the powerful currents of anxiety and despair, and from drowning in our fears and doubts.

Though we've experienced our share of small blessings, often at a price, He has shown us His love by showering us with favour in our daily walk with Him. Obedience is the key to unlocking peace and prosperity in our lives.

But what does obedience look like in daily life? It means choosing to trust Him, even when we don't understand His ways. It means listening to His voice, however softly it may whisper.

It means surrendering our will to His, even when it's hard. And it means following His commands, no matter how difficult they may seem.

The Lord once revealed a vision to me—a giant hand, signifying that the entire world is in His grasp. He sees all things and hears all things, including the cries of His people from every angle. God hears the pleas of both the virtuous and the wicked, judging all with impartial justice.

God yearns to reign supreme in the hearts of those who call Him by His name. He implores us to keep our hands in His, so He can carry us through every trial and tribulation.

During those tough times, between the rocks and the hard places, we will discover joy like never before—a joy that's rooted in our trust in Him.

In a world filled with turmoil and dangers, He has left us with His perfect peace. He urges us to place our burdens in His hands, and we will never lack for anything.

God does not force His will upon us; instead, He gently guides us. As we put our faith in Him, we will find that He is our rock, our refuge in times of trouble.

We must learn to listen to God's gentle voice. It often whispers in the dark, uncertain times when doubt threatens to overwhelm us. It's a call to surrender our desires, ambitions, and fears. We must exchange them for His peace that transcends our understanding.

As the prophet Isaiah reminded us, God's ways are higher than ours, soaring like an eagle above the mundane routines of our daily lives. His plans are far superior to our limited human designs, which are often narrow-minded and short-sighted.

Like a master architect, God's blueprints are complex and detailed. They account for every contingency. Our plans are like rough sketches, full of errors. For instance, who could have foreseen the rise of the Israelites from slavery to nationhood?

Or, the transformation of the apostle Paul from a fierce persecutor to a passionate advocate for Christ? God's ways are not only higher but also often unpredictable, defying human logic and understanding. Yet, it is in surrendering to His superior plans that we find true purpose and fulfillment.

When we obey His will, He opens doors we never thought possible. He leads us to great places where we can fulfill our true potential. For example, consider Joseph's story. His brothers sold him into slavery. He rose to become a powerful leader in Egypt.

He rescued his family and community from the brink of starvation, providing them with a new lease on life. This remarkable act of salvation was not a coincidence, but a direct result of surrendering to God's divine plan. When we put our trust in a higher power, we open ourselves up to a world of possibilities.

Like a farmer who tilts his soil to receive the nourishing rains, we too can prepare ourselves to receive the abundance that God has in store for us. These opportunities may appear as breakthroughs.

Like a sudden downpour on parched earth, they can bring new life to our situations. They may be solutions we never thought possible. They may seem to defy the odds. But they are the result of surrendering to God's infinite wisdom.

God's plans unlock new paths for us. We can see this in the lives of biblical heroes. Take the story of Moses, for instance. He went from being a shepherd to leading the Israelites out of slavery in Egypt.

God's plans turned his simple life into a remarkable journey. As we trust in God, we can expect similar surprises, too.

We often struggle to comprehend how God's plans will unfold, leaving us with more questions than answers. Nevertheless, we can have faith that His intentions are good, even when we can't see the bigger picture.

We can take comfort in knowing that God's plans are not limited by our understanding. He can turn any situation around, no matter how impossible it seems. Just like a small seed can grow into a mighty tree, our tiny acts of faith can lead to incredible outcomes.

By trusting God, we open ourselves up to his limitless power and potential.

This confidence comes from many examples. They show that those who obey God's will see extraordinary results. Take, for instance, the remarkable story of David, a humble young shepherd boy who would eventually become the King of Israel.

In a time when social hierarchy was deeply ingrained, it defied logic that a humble shepherd boy would be handpicked by God to lead His people. Yet, God's eye saw beyond human limits. It found in David a potential that others overlooked.

God's choice of David teaches us to look beyond our limitations. We often judge people by what they seem to be, not by what they can become. But God sees the full potential in each of us, even when we don't see it ourselves. When we trust Him, we can rise above our doubts and fears, just like David did.

The young shepherd David's faith in God emboldened him. He confronted the giant Goliath, whose size and roar had paralyzed the Israelite army. David's trust in God's power coursed through his veins like a river of steel, fortifying his resolve to take on the monstrous warrior.

As he approached Goliath, the air was thick with tension, the only sound was the rustling of leaves and the heavy breathing of the giant.

David's stone, hurled with precision and faith, struck Goliath's forehead, toppling the giant like a felled oak. As news of this miraculous victory spread, it sparked hope in God's people, who had lived in fear under Philistine rule.

David's triumphant cry echoed throughout the land. It shattered the chains of despair and oppression. It cemented his legacy as a hero of faith and courage.

But God chose David, a young shepherd from Bethlehem, to be the king of Israel. This unexpected choice surprised David. He doubted his skills to lead the nation. After all, he was still a teenager, tasked with protecting his family's flock from lions and bears, not governing a kingdom.

Yet, God saw beyond David's unassuming appearance and modest background, which seemed ordinary to the human eye. He searched his heart. There, a strong faith, unwavering courage, and a sense of justice dwelled. These would make him a legendary leader.

David's journey to kingship was not without its challenges. As a young man, he faced fierce opposition from King Saul, who had been rejected by God. Saul was jealous of David's rising popularity and feared he would lose his throne.

He relentlessly pursued David, wanting to kill him. But David's faith in God's protection never wavered. In their deadly conflict, David stayed loyal to Saul. He rejected chances to take the throne and get revenge.

For instance, when Saul entered the cave, David could have slain him. But he chose to spare his life, citing his reverence for God's anointed king. This loyalty and self-control show David's deep trust in God's power. It sustained him on his dangerous journey.

David's loyalty was tested when he spared Saul's life in the dark, eerie cave of En Gedi. Ancient Israelites used it to escape the scorching sun. Saul, unaware that his greatest enemy lurked in the shadows, had wandered into the cave. This gave David the chance to avenge past wrongs.

But David's men, driven by a desire for revenge, urged him to kill Saul, reminding him of the many times Saul had sought to destroy him. Yet, David refused, citing a moral obligation to respect God's chosen leader, saying, "I will not touch the Lord's anointed."

This decision showed mercy. It also showed David's faith. He upheld its sacred principles, even when it was hard.

CHAPTER 3
DO YOU FEEL UNWORTHY?

When God breathed life into Adam, He imparted a part of His spirit, making Adam a living soul. A sacred connection joins Adam to God, a birthright we receive. But life's challenges can make us forget our true value. We then see ourselves as mere bodies, not living souls.

We often question our self-worth because of the painful experiences we've gone through. Take, for example, a child who was constantly criticized by their parents. These hurtful words can linger, leading to feelings of guilt and shame that can last a lifetime.

We might remember every detail of that embarrassing moment in front of our classmates, replaying it in our minds like a broken record.

As a result, anxiety starts to creep in, making us wonder if we're truly good enough. These negative emotions distract us from our strengths and talents, causing us to fixate on our flaws instead.

It's like trying to focus on the beauty of a sunset while being consumed by the darkness of a storm cloud. As a result, we struggle to accept ourselves as God's beloved children, just as He lovingly created us to be.

God has given us spiritual gifts to glorify Him. When we accept Jesus and receive the Holy Spirit, we can use these gifts to serve others and find joy in our lives. Unfortunately, many of us forget how to use these gifts, letting past hurts and failures define us.

Instead, we must remember that our identity comes from God, not our mistakes. By focusing on our spiritual gifts, we can heal and see ourselves as God does.

In the Bible, God says He will give us a new heart and a new spirit. This means He can restore our connection to Him and help us remember our identity. Remember, our worth doesn't come from our past or what others think of us.

It comes from God, who loves us and wants to bring us back to Himself. He wants us to live free from the weight of shame and guilt, using our spiritual gifts to serve and glorify Him.

According to *Joel 2:28, God will pour out His Spirit on all people, allowing us to prophesy, dream, and see visions.*

On the day of Pentecost, a pivotal moment in Christian history, God fulfilled His promise to empower believers with spiritual gifts, making this blessing available to all generations.

These gifts, graciously bestowed upon us by God, are irrevocable - a permanent endowment that cannot be revoked or cancelled.

However, the efficacy of these gifts depends on who we choose to guide us: the Holy Spirit, who inspires and directs us towards good, or demons, who seek to corrupt and mislead us.

The apostle Paul reminds us in 1 Corinthians 12:1-3 that spiritual gifts are manifestations of God's grace.

Let them be guided by the divine yet beware of the whispers of darkness that seek to lead them astray. The thin line between the sacred and the profane demands we exercise discernment, incorporating prayer as a vital component in our spiritual journeys.

Consider the ancient tale of Solomon, who, blessed with divine wisdom, still succumbed to the allure of dark powers, illustrating the precarious nature of this balance.

As we navigate our spiritual paths, we must remain vigilant, recognizing that even the most well-intentioned among us can fall prey to the diabolical. The consequences of such a downfall can be catastrophic, as seen in the biblical account of Adam and Eve, whose disobedience allowed darkness to enter the world.

It is only through the steady practice of discernment, rooted in prayer and a deep understanding of the divine, that we can safeguard our spiritual growth and avoid the pitfalls of darkness.

We must acknowledge that spiritual gifts can be valuable assets in our spiritual battles. Yet, we must not become complacent, for our adversaries are cunning and relentless.

The scriptures remind us that even the strongest among us can stumble, as seen in the case of Peter, who, despite his loyalty to Jesus, momentarily denied his Lord, highlighting the persistent threat of darkness.

God wants us to use our spiritual gifts to serve others, not to seek praise or recognition. He gives us these gifts to build up the church and bring people closer to Him. When we use our gifts with the right motives, we honour God and bless people. This is how we show God's love to the world.

Using our spiritual gifts, guided by the Holy Spirit, helps us. We begin to understand God's plan for our lives. We walk in faith, not fear. By repenting and accepting Jesus, believers activate these gifts for God's glory.

We must pray for wisdom to use our gifts wisely. The Holy Spirit helps us understand how to use our gifts to benefit others, not ourselves. When we let God guide us, our gifts bring joy and comfort to those around us.

We become humble servants, pointing people to God, not seeking to attract attention to ourselves.

But, if demonic forces gain control over them, they can corrupt these divine gifts, twisting them for dark purposes. They may use their charismatic leadership to deceive and manipulate others, leading to chaos and devastation.

For instance, consider the example of false prophets throughout history who have misused their spiritual influence to spread lies and confusion.

When believers let their gifts shine, they bring hope to a broken world. They become light in the darkness, pointing the way to Jesus. This is how God uses us to change lives and bring people to Himself.

By staying close to God, we keep our gifts pure and focused on helping others, not ourselves.

When believers, like the apostle Paul, are led astray by demonic forces, they can fall prey to selfish ambitions and pride, causing them to stray from their original purpose.

This not only harms their spiritual growth but also affects the entire community, much like a single rotten apple can spoil the entire basket.

When believers use their spiritual gifts for the right reasons, they follow God's plan. This plan is to serve others, not to gain power or fame. Serving others shows God's love and care for them. By doing so, we become a blessing to those around us.

Satan often tries to mimic God's gifts. He leads people astray with false promises of power and spiritual awareness. Many seek spiritual power in the wrong places. These include meditation, yoga, and the occult.

They can open doors to destructive forces. These practices may help for a while. But they lead away from God's truth.

God's gifts are not just for us, but for others too. When we use them to help others, we show God's love in action. This love changes lives and brings people closer to God.

Satan hates this and tries to stop us from using our gifts for good. He wants us to use them for selfish reasons, like seeking power or fame.

Satan's tricks can be hard to spot. He makes evil look good and good look evil. Many people get fooled by his lies. That's why we need to test everything against God's Word.

We must stay close to God and pray for wisdom. Through prayer, we can tell the difference between God's gifts and Satan's tricks.

Satan's tactics also include attacking children. He plants seeds of self-doubt and fear from a young age. This can lead to a lifetime of feeling unworthy. His goal is to silence the potential within them to bring hope and change to the world. This attack can cause children to reject their true potential. It leads to a cycle of rejection, anger, and destructive behaviours.

Satan tries to drive a wedge between us and God's unconditional love. He constantly whispers deceitful lies into our ears, convincing us that we're not good enough, that we've fallen short of divine expectations.

These lies sink deep into our hearts, filling us with overwhelming shame and suffocating guilt. As a result, we start to feel unworthy of God's love, like we're too flawed, too broken, or too sinful to receive His forgiveness and grace.

God holds a distinct perspective on us. He sees us as valuable and loved, regardless of our past. He can use our brokenness to shape us into vessels for His purpose. In God's kingdom, we are all wanted and cherished.

God's love sets us free from Satan's trap. It helps us see our true worth. We need to focus on God's voice, not Satan's lies. His love gives us the courage to overcome shame and guilt. In His kingdom, we are precious and loved, not defined by our mistakes.

God's love gives us a new identity. We are no longer trapped by our past mistakes. His love helps us reject the lies of Satan and embrace our true self-worth. As we focus on God's voice, we break free from shame and guilt.

We start to see ourselves as God sees us - valued, loved, and worthy of forgiveness and grace.

Sometimes, adopted children may experience feelings of rejection when they meet their biological parents. This emotional turmoil can be overwhelming, leaving them wondering why they were given up or abandoned. However, it's essential to remember that even in pain, there is a purpose.

As the Bible says, *"And we know that in all things God works for the good of those who love him, who have been called according to his purpose"* (Romans 8:28). For instance, consider the story of Moses, who was placed in the river in a basket by his biological mother to save his life.

An Egyptian princess found him and raised him. Despite his complex upbringing, Moses went on to lead the Israelites out of slavery and become a great leader.

God's love empowers adopted children to overcome their past. They can rise above feelings of rejection and shame. As they focus on God's love, they begin to see their biological parents' decision as a catalyst for good. This shift in perspective helps them discover their true purpose and identity in God.

In my own life, I have a unique story. I didn't grow up with my biological family, but I was fortunate to be raised in a home that valued spiritual growth. This laid a strong foundation in God's Word, teaching me to trust in His sovereignty even when faced with challenging emotions.

Through my experiences, I've come to understand that God can turn even the most painful situations into blessings, revealing His glory and love in ways we never thought possible.

I accepted Jesus as my Saviour at a young age. This helped me understand God's love and plan for my life. God's love for me is absolute, without strings attached. He wants me to know my true worth in Him.

This understanding gave me confidence and helped me overcome feelings of rejection.

God has allowed me to meet my siblings to guide them towards truth and wisdom. Through His love, I have been able to reach them, shining light into their darkness.

My journey has shown me that God's plan is always good, even when it is hard to understand. My faith empowers me, giving me direction to make a difference.

Joel 2: 28 tells us that:

It shall come to pass afterward, that I will pour out my spirit upon all flesh; and your sons and daughters shall prophesy, your old men shall dream dreams, and your young men shall see visions.

Romans, 11.29 tells us that:

For the Gifts and Calling of God are without repentance...

Satan understands humans have an innate longing for spiritual enlightenment. He's actively working to mislead us by filling this void with counterfeit experiences, leaving us feeling unfulfilled and empty.

His goal is to distract us from the true source of spiritual awareness, which is God.

God's plan for me is to transform my struggles into a beacon of hope for others. He has entrusted me with a powerful voice, empowering me to spread His life-changing message to everyone around me.

My siblings, who have witnessed my journey firsthand, are just the starting point.

As I share my story, I hope to ignite a spark in others, encouraging them to seek God's guidance and wisdom. For instance, when I was at my lowest point, I found solace in His words, and it completely turned my life around.

I believe that by being vulnerable and open about my experiences, I can help others find their path to redemption and healing. By doing so, I hope to create a ripple effect, inspiring a chain reaction of kindness, compassion, and love that resonates deeply within my community and beyond.

In contrast, God's spirit is accessible to anyone who genuinely seeks Him. When we humbly ask, He generously pours out His Spirit, granting us wisdom, inspiring dreams, and revealing visions. This empowerment enables us to comprehend His grand plan and live a life that has a profound impact.

God wants us to understand that He empowers us, giving us direction to make a difference. He pours out His spirit upon all flesh, making our sons and daughters prophesy, our old men dream dreams, and our young men see visions. The gifts and calling of God are without repentance.

God's plan is not confined to my journey, nor is it limited to my immediate circle. He has a grand design to use the bride of Christ as an instrument of change, making a profound and lasting impact on the world around us.

Through the believer's unwavering faith, we can be a beacon of inspiration to those who are disheartened, offer solace to the sorrowful, and bring a glimmer of hope to those who are struggling to find their way.

He plans to rouse a generation that walks in His power. With hearts overflowing, they will bring light to darker places, speak life into dead situations, and restore hope to broken lives. We can be that generation, united by a common purpose to spread love, kindness, and justice.

As we align our lives with God's compassionate heart, His gentle yet powerful presence begins to transform us from the inside out. Like clay moulded by a skilled potter, He shapes us into the people He created us to be, preparing us for the significant task that lies ahead.

This transformation is not just a superficial change, but a deep, profound one that touches every aspect of our being.

It's a process that requires patience, trust, and surrender, but the result is well worth it - we become more like Him, reflecting His love, kindness, and wisdom to a world in desperate need of it.

Revelation of Truth

I have made you a messenger to send my Truth to all nations. I use your determination, and persistence to spread my truths, my love, and power to all who will hear my voice. I will send you out to many more nations to teach my Truths.

I look at the heartstrings to see what makes you worthy. My blood was sacrificed on the cross and your repentance has made you worthy. I showed you my cross to show you that I died for you, for your sins and because of this you have been found worthy.

Stand on the Word of God and see the salvation of your King. The enemy attacks the soul, see it for what and who it is and cast him away from you. I have given you weapons against the enemy. Use them!!!

CHAPTER 4
BE TRUE TO YOURSELF

We often see in others what isn't there. We wear masks to hide our true selves. We seek acceptance and fear rejection. But living behind a mask is exhausting and disconnects us from our identity.

To gain acceptance, we may pretend to be someone we're not. This creates a gap between who we are and who we want others to think we are. Pretending sparks inner turmoil, draining our energy and resolve.

Embracing flaws and unique traits defines authentic living. It's about recognizing our strengths and weaknesses. When we're true to ourselves, we break free from the weight of pretending. We can finally be at peace with who we are, without apology or excuse.

Breaking free from the need for approval is crucial. Seeking validation from others makes us inauthentic. We disconnect from our true feelings, thoughts, and desires. This separation often leads to loneliness. We feel distant from our true selves.

We need to stop seeking approval from others. Approval is not the same as self-acceptance. We must focus on our self-worth; not what others think of us. When we do, we'll feel more confident and grounded.

When we're honest with ourselves, we can start to heal. Letting go of our masks means embracing our strengths and weaknesses. It means not feeling the pressure to be perfect. This journey requires courage.

But the reward is profound. It is the freedom to live as our true selves, unburdened by pretending.

Living behind a facade can lead us to believe the lies we present to others. We might get compliments like, "You're so lucky" or "You have it all together." But we know we're struggling to maintain this image. Honesty about our weaknesses and fears frees us. We no longer feel the pressure to appear flawless.

The stress of a fake image eventually catches up with us. It can cause anxiety, depression, or even physical illness. Let's drop the act. We can then focus on our well-being. This will help us find true happiness, not a shallow, appearance-based version.

We often sense disharmony in others. We feel when something is off, even if we can't explain it. We might act confident to seem successful. But we know it's not genuine. Many of us share this struggle, appearing calm while battling fears and doubts.

When we live a lie, our words and actions no longer match our true thoughts and feelings. This disconnect can lead to self-doubt, as we wonder if we're the only ones feeling this way. But we are not alone; many people put on a brave face to hide their insecurities.

Living authentically frees us from artificial constraints. It lets us connect deeply and be true to ourselves. When we drop the mask and show our true feelings, we build stronger bonds. It allows others to see the real us, flaws and all.

Living authentically also helps us develop a sense of self-acceptance. We learn to love ourselves, flaws and all. This self-love gives us the courage to take risks and pursue our passions. It lets us live life on our terms, not according to someone else's expectations.

When we are honest about our struggles, we create a safe space for others to do the same. By being open and vulnerable, we inspire others to let their guard down too.

Honesty creates a ripple effect. When we share our struggles, others feel comfortable doing the same. This openness builds trust and strengthens relationships. By being truthful, we create a sense of community where everyone feels safe to be themselves.

Authentic living is contagious, and it can start a chain reaction of honesty and trust. This lets us build deep relationships based on mutual understanding, not looks. Pretending to impress others is a heavy burden.

When we stop, we can finally relax and be ourselves. This authenticity frees us to pursue our passions and dreams. It lifts the pressure of pretending and empowers us to embrace life with confidence and joy.

Embracing authenticity also helps us learn from our mistakes. When we're open about our struggles, we can ask for help and guidance from others. This fosters growth and self improvement, ending the need to pretend to be perfect.

If we admit our weaknesses, we can build our strengths and improve. This journey of self discovery is lifelong. But it has purpose and direction. It helps us grow in deeply fulfilling ways.

Living authentically also strengthens our sense of self. When we stop comparing ourselves to others, we feel a sense of belonging. We connect with people who appreciate us for who we are.

Living Authentically According to God's Word

To be true to ourselves, we must follow God's Word. We must align our identity, actions, and purpose with the teachings of Scripture. Here are some key steps:

1. Recognize Your Identity in Christ - **Scripture Reference: **

"So, God created mankind in his own image, in the image of God he created them; male and female he created them." (Genesis 1:27)

- Your identity is rooted in being created in the image of God. As a believer, your identity is further shaped by your relationship with

Christ. Knowing who you are in Christ helps you live authentically. It lets you embrace the person God created you to be.

2. Seek God's Will

- **Scripture Reference: ** *"Trust in the LORD with all your heart and lean not on your own understanding; in all your ways submit to him, and he will make your paths straight." (Proverbs 3:5-6)*

- Being true to yourself involves seeking and following God's will for your life. Trust in His guidance, pray for wisdom, and be open to His direction, even when it challenges your desires.

3. Live According to God's Commandments

- **Scripture Reference: ** *"If you love me, keep my commands." (John 14:15)*

- A life true to yourself, according to God's Word, strives to live according to His commandments. *This involves loving God with all your heart, soul, and mind, and loving your neighbour as yourself (Matthew 22:37-39).*

4. RENEW YOUR MIND

**Scripture Reference: ** *"Do not conform to the pattern of this world but be transformed by the renewing of your mind. Then you will be able to test and approve what God's will is— his good, pleasing and perfect will."* (Romans 12:2)

Allow God to transform your thinking. Immerse yourself in Scripture, allowing the Holy Spirit to guide your thoughts, and reject worldly influences that conflict with God's truth.

5. Embrace Humility and Dependence on God

**SCRIPTURE REFERENCE: ** *"Humble yourselves, therefore, under God's mighty hand, that he may lift you up in due time."* (1 Peter 5:6)

True authenticity before God requires humility. Acknowledge your need for God's grace and guidance in every area of your life. Depend on Him rather than your strength.

6.Build a Strong Support Network

Surround yourself with people who encourage and support your faith. Join a community of believers, such as a church or Bible study group, where you can grow together.

7. Practice: Forgiveness and Mercy

Scripture Reference: *"Be kind and compassionate to one another, forgiving each other, just as in Christ God forgave you." (Ephesians 4:32)*

Let go of grudges and resentments. Show mercy to others, just as God has shown mercy to you. This breaks down barriers and creates a path for deeper relationships with God and others.

Acknowledge that you are not perfect. Recognize that you make mistakes and can hurt others. Be willing to ask for forgiveness when you have wronged someone.

8. Practice: Forgiveness and Gratitude

Express thanks to God for the good things in your life. Focus on His blessings, not your problems. Gratitude shifts your attention from what's lacking to what you already have. It helps you see that God is always with you, even in difficult times.

Scripture Reference: *"Get rid of all bitterness, rage and anger, brawling and slander, along with every form of malice. Be kind and compassionate to one another, forgiving each other, just as in Christ God forgave you." (Ephesians 4:31-32)*

Let go of grudges and resentments. Forgive others as God forgave you. Show kindness and compassion to those around you. Cultivate a heart of gratitude by thanking God for His blessings.

9. Reflect Christ's Character

*SCRIPTURE REFERENCE: ** *"You were taught, with regard to your former way of life, to put off your old self, which is being corrupted by its deceitful desires; to be made new in the attitude of your minds; and to put on the new self, created to be like God in true righteousness and holiness."* (Ephesians 4:22-24)

Becoming true to yourself in the light of God's Word means becoming more like Christ. This involves putting off your old self and embracing the new life that Christ offers, characterized by righteousness and holiness.

10. Bear the Fruit of the Spirit

**SCRIPTURE REFERENCE: ** *"But the fruit of the Spirit is love, joy, peace, forbearance, kindness, goodness, faithfulness, gentleness and self-control. Against such things, there is no law."* (Galatians 5:22-23)

As you grow in your relationship with God, the Holy Spirit will produce fruit in your life that reflects God's character. Living according to these virtues is a true expression of who you are in Christ.

11. Seek First the Kingdom of God

**SCRIPTURE REFERENCE: ** *"But seek first his kingdom and his righteousness, and all these things will be given to you as well."* (Matthew 6:33)

Prioritizing God's kingdom and righteousness ensures that your life is centered on what truly matters. This focus helps you stay true to your God-given purpose and identity.

12. Love Others as Yourself

**SCRIPTURE REFERENCE: ** *"A new command I give you: Love one another. As I have loved you, so you must love one another."* *(John 13:34)*

Living authentically according to God's Word involves expressing love towards others, as this is a core commandment of the Christian faith. Loving others reflects God's love and is an essential part of being true to yourself as a follower of Christ.

13. Be a Witness to God's Truth

**SCRIPTURE REFERENCE: ** *"You are the light of the world. A town built on a hill cannot be hidden."* *(Matthew 5:14)*

Part of being true to yourself in a biblical sense is living in a way that reflects God's truth to the world. Your life should be a testament to the reality of God's love, grace, and truth.

By aligning your life with these biblical principles, you become true to yourself in a way that honors God and fulfills His purpose for your life.

CHAPTER 5

DO YOU FEEL INSIGNIFICANT IN YOUR FAMILY?

Reflection and Encouragement

Some of us feel insignificant within our family, often the last to know about crucial situations, events, and updates. This exclusion breeds fear, mistrust, and confusion, leaving us feeling isolated and disconnected.

Though we might try to convince ourselves it's not a big deal, deep down, it hurts to be left out. This sense of exclusion can make us question our importance within the family, leading to self-doubt, low self-esteem, and a feeling of not belonging. We may start to believe that our thoughts and contributions don't matter, which can drive us to withdraw emotionally.

Hiding these feelings can affect our behaviour. We might pull back from family gatherings or stop sharing our thoughts and emotions, deepening our sense of isolation. This withdrawal can strain relationships, making it harder to reconnect and communicate openly.

To maintain our mental and emotional health, it's crucial to remember our inherent value within the family. Each of us is here because we bring unique contributions—whether it's joy, laughter, a sense of peace, or support during tough times.

Recognizing this starts with small steps. Speak up when you feel left out and share your thoughts and feelings with a trusted family member. This fosters inclusion and breaks down the walls of insignificance.

We often overlook our strengths and the positive impact we have on our family. This oversight can make us feel like we're not good enough, thinking that others in our family are more important or talented. By focusing on our unique qualities and what we bring to the table, we can shift our mindset and recognize our true value.

Forgiving ourselves and others is essential, as holding onto bitterness drains our energy and further isolates us. Focusing on the positive aspects of our family can create a more harmonious environment, where everyone feels valued and supported.

In some families, anger simmers beneath the surface, possibly as a shared trait. However, our empathetic hearts allow us to resonate with others' pain and underlying desires. This sensitivity transcends bloodlines, shaping our interactions with the world around us.

Our openness to understanding helps us navigate difficult emotions, calming anger by validating each other's feelings. This creates a safe space for honest conversations, allowing us to address underlying issues instead of letting them fester.

God shines His light on the lowly and forgotten, those whom the family may overlook. He does this so others may find their way to Him. Truth, steadfastness, and persistence are qualities that flourish in the believer who loves God.

These qualities, however, can stir jealousy and stubbornness in others, leading to resentment. In such cases, only God can intervene. When we show love to the overlooked, we reflect God's love.

We can do this by listening to their stories and validating their emotions, which quiets anger and opens doors for healing. By doing so, we create a safe space where everyone feels seen and heard.

Families may label us as failures, but others see us differently. Some recognize the great love within us, which is of great value in the kingdom of God. God looks at the heart, knowing its purity and the depth of our love for Him despite the hardships and tests we face.

These trials are often purposeful, teaching us through trial and error. If we seek clarity from God's Word, He will provide the answers we need. Reflect on your life's achievements, trusting that God will guide your loved ones back to Him in His time. His word will not return void, even when circumstances seem impossible.

Our children, spiritual beings in search of God's love, will eventually find it. Continue praying for them, for God has not forgotten them. He hears their cries and will honor our prayers when the time is right. They may appear hardened by life's trials, but they are being refined, not yet ready to emerge as new creations.

Success is not measured by material wealth but by spiritual growth. In heaven, spiritual matters are held in higher regard. Seek first the kingdom of God and His righteousness, and everything else will be added to you. Keep your focus on Him, study the Word, and pray continually, and He will honour your efforts.

We are placed in our families to guide those who are lost and searching. We are where we need to be, and it is our task to understand how we fit in. As believers, our steps are ordered by the Lord, provided we seek His will for our lives. Those who belong to the Father are cleansed through trials—through fire, water, and blood.

God uproots us, shakes us, and sometimes rattles us to move us, only to settle us on firm ground. He alone uproots the weeds and plants the flowers. Once they bloom, they are ready to be gathered.

God teaches us patience as we wait for Him to respond to our prayers. We may feel stuck, but He is shaping us for His purpose. Our part is to trust and obey, for He knows the right time to act. Meanwhile, we learn to surrender our will to His and find peace in the process.

God's children must be awakened to do His work and placed on solid ground. The labourers are few because they lack knowledge and the necessary tools to fulfill His mission. God chooses to use ordinary people like us to carry out His extraordinary work.

We are His vessels, filled with purpose and direction. Our role is to obey and trust Him completely. He seeks to increase our faith, but we must be willing to let go of our doubts and fears.

God speaks to us in a gentle voice, guiding us through life's challenges. He uses our struggles to strengthen us, making us fit for His purpose. As we follow Him, we learn to let go of our plans and desires and trust in His perfect timing.

As we surrender to Him, He shapes us into the people He designed us to be, using us to impact the lives of those around us.

God works through our weaknesses to show His power. He uses our failures to teach us valuable lessons. As we surrender to Him, He fills us with courage and confidence to serve others. His goal is to make us bold witnesses of His love and mercy.

Revelation of Truth

"My blood has set you free, and I have given you the opportunity to know your loved ones; this is not a mistake. You are exactly where you should be, as ordained before the foundation of the world. Your connection is not only through familial blood but also through My Blood, which redeems sins.

Do not let Satan steal your peace. My peace I leave with you. Look to Me as the finisher of your faith, knowing that I have all things under control. You are no longer a child; it is time to mature in My Word. Move beyond the basics and delve deeper into the truths I have for you.

As you study My Word, I will open your eyes to new understandings, revealing mysteries to those who diligently seek Me with their whole heart. You have faced troubled waters and walked on them as I held your hand.

I have kept you from harm, and the blessings you received, though they came with a price, were just the beginning. Greater blessings await you as you continue to obey My voice.

Keep your hand in My Hand, and I will carry you through. You will experience joy like never before. My peace I leave with you in a world filled with chaos and turmoil. My hand is vast, holding the entire world within My grasp. I see and hear all things, including the cries of My people. I hear the cries of both the just and the unjust.

I rain justly upon all humanity, but I long to reign in the hearts of those who call Me by My name. Keep your peace with Me, place it in My hands, and you will never lack anything.

My people do not be afraid of the darkness that surrounds you. I am the light that shines bright in the darkest night. I will guide you through the storm, and you will come out stronger on the other side.

Hold on to Me, and I will hold on to you. You will not be shaken, for I am your Rock. I will give you rest when you are weary, and My presence will comfort you in times of sorrow."

CHAPTER 6
REBELLION COSTS LIVES

✱✱The Journey from Fear to Love

When I first experienced salvation, my perception of God was that of a strict, unforgiving authority figure, demanding unwavering obedience. I believed that living a holy life meant adhering to a rigid set of rules, leaving no room for spontaneity or joy.

This view was shaped by the teachings of the church where I spent my formative years, where the focus was more on the consequences of disobedience than on inspiring hope or love.

I remember feeling an overwhelming sense of responsibility, as if my eternal destiny hinged on my ability to follow every commandment to the letter. This perception of God filled me with fear and guilt, trapping me in a cycle where I believed that one misstep could lead to eternal damnation.

My faith felt like a burden, a constant weight on my shoulders, and I longed for the freedom and joy that seemed like impossible dreams.

The sermons we heard were like dark clouds, filled with warnings of fiery brimstone and endless agony, rarely offering a glimpse of God's mercy or compassion. The preachers used fear as a tool to keep us in line, raising their voices, yelling, and painting vivid pictures of eternal suffering.

This approach created a chasm between us and the gentle, loving God they claimed to serve, leading us to see Him more as a wrathful judge than a benevolent guide.

The church I attended growing up emphasized the fear of hell over the love of God. We were constantly reminded that without salvation, we were doomed to suffer eternal damnation.

As a young person, this message was overwhelming and disheartening, and the fear that gripped our hearts as children stayed with us long after we left the church. It echoed in our minds whenever we faced difficult choices or made mistakes, leaving us feeling like we were never good enough.

Feeling that I could never meet the standards required to avoid hell, I became rebellious. Salvation seemed like something reserved for the older generation, and I distanced myself from the church, seeing it as joyless and restrictive.

I do not remember feeling any faith, only the terror the messages installed in me. Every week I felt the constant cycle of fear and guilt. Eventually I learned to turn this part of church services off, and only enjoy the worship – the singing.

This fear eventually turned into anger and resentment towards the church and its teachings. I questioned why the focus was on hellfire and damnation instead of God's love and mercy.

Why were we taught to fear God rather than to love Him? This rebellion led me to pursue my own path, doing what I wanted without regard for the consequences. However, this path left me feeling empty and unfulfilled.

It wasn't until I encountered real love—God's love—that my perspective began to change. I started to see people who had a genuine connection with God, who didn't fear Him but loved Him.

They showed me that faith could be joyful, not restrictive, and that life with God was about freedom, not fear.

In my late teens, in that little church front in Scarborough I finally began to understand the true nature of God. I realized that a relationship with Him could bring joy, peace, and fulfillment, and that it was based on love and trust, not fear and obligation.

I started to build a new foundation, one based on my own experiences and interactions with God. I learned to listen to His gentle voice, guiding me toward a path of love and compassion.

As I matured in my faith, I began to notice profound changes in my daily interactions. For example, I started responding to life's irritations with patience and empathy, rather than allowing anger or frustration to control me.

On the busy subway as I stood too close to others, I would take a deep breath and let the annoyance dissipate, focusing instead on the beauty of the world around me.

During tense conversations, I paused to consider the other person's perspective and responded with love and kindness.

These subtle shifts led to remarkable improvements in my relationships, as I felt a deep sense of unity with those around me.

When we sing to the Lord, we are precious in His sight, for He sees our dedication and determination to please Him. No matter what challenges we face, God is always there to help us through.

When we call upon Him in times of peace or danger, He answers. His faithfulness is a testimony to His love and care for us. As I sang to the Lord, I felt His love surround me, filling my heart with joy. I knew He was with me, guiding me through life's ups and downs, and this realization filled me with confidence.

Life is a journey that requires preparation because situations can arise without notice. We will travel through the valleys of life, but with each valley, we can feel His presence and know that we are not alone.

The key to a victorious life is to cultivate a deep and abiding relationship with God, marked by consistent prayer, watchfulness, a commitment to living a holy life, and obedience to His voice.

Imagine God as a skilled gardener tending to a once-neglected garden. He carefully uproots the damaged, abused, and neglected areas of our lives, just as a gardener removes weeds to make way for new growth.

He cleanses us, washing away the dirt and grime that has accumulated, and fills us with His Holy Spirit, much like a master potter refines and perfects a delicate vase. As we surrender to His will, He transforms us into pure vessels, fit for His glory and purposes.

God works in us, using our struggles to shape us into what He wants us to be. His goal is to make us more like Jesus. Through our struggles, we learn to lean on Him and trust in His power.

We become stronger as we face challenges, just as our muscles grow stronger when we exercise them. Every time we cry out to God in desperation, He humbles us, and His Spirit stirs within us, refining and healing our wounded souls.

Consider the story of the prophet Jonah, who stubbornly resisted God's call, yet God still used his determination to spread His message to the people of Nineveh. Similarly, God can take our persistence, our unyielding determination, and even our stubbornness, and transform them into powerful tools for His glory.

Through this process, we are remade, our hearts purified, so that we may reflect His character and be used mightily by Him.

God delights in using our weaknesses to showcase His strength. He weaves our mistakes into a beautiful tapestry of redemption, turning our brokenness into a masterpiece of His love. As we surrender our struggles, He mends our shattered dreams and shapes us into vessels for His honor.

These qualities, when surrendered to Him, can move mountains in the kingdom of God. He needs servants who will stand firm to the end, who will not waver in their faith or commitment to His will.

Rebellion may have its costs, but redemption is always within reach through the boundless mercy of God's grace. Consider the story of the prodigal son, who squandered his inheritance and lost his way, yet was welcomed back with open arms by his forgiving father—a poignant illustration of God's unwavering love.

No matter how far we stray, God's love is always ready to bring us back, heal our wounds, and set us on the path of righteousness. The psalmist aptly conveys this sentiment: "*The Lord is merciful and gracious, slow to anger and abounding in steadfast love*" (Psalm 103:8).

This understanding brings solace to those who have faltered, illuminating the darkness with the warm light of redemption.

Revelation of Truth

Keep praying and seeking My face, and I will give you more songs to sing of My glory. Those who hear will be healed and set free.

I have seen your heartache, your tears, and I have heard your pleas to hold back the songs I give to you. But I say to you, be faithful in the small things, and I will give you the larger things.

I will bring what is incomplete to completion. Do not let Satan steal your peace; My peace I leave with you. Look to Me as the finisher of your faith. I have all things under My control. You are no longer a child; it is time to feast on the meat of My Word.

No more milk for the seasoned warrior. Study, and study some more. As you read My Word, I will open your eyes of understanding and reveal to you the mysteries hidden in My Word.

You have seen troubled waters and walked on them as I held your hand. I have kept you from harm. The blessings you received, though they came with a price, were small in comparison to what I have in store for you as you continue to obey My voice.

Keep your hand in Mine. I have shown you My hand, vast and powerful. I hold the whole world in My grasp. As I turn My hand, I see all things and hear all cries—the cries of the just and the unjust.

I rain justly upon all humanity, but I long to reign in the hearts of those who call Me by My name.

Keep your hand in Mine, and I will carry you through. You will know joy like never before. My peace I leave with you in a world filled with turmoil and greed.

FOR THE SHATTERED SOUL

Keep your peace with Me, place it in My hands, and you will never lack anything.

CHAPTER 7
BULLIED AND ABUSED

Reflecting on your life's journey, you'll notice pivotal moments that have shaped your path, many of which were influenced by your thoughts and actions. If you were bullied or abused in your youth, those experiences likely left scars that still affect you today.

The painful memories of being belittled or intimidated may resurface, leading to self-doubt, anxiety, and a fear of intimacy, which hinders your ability to form trusting relationships. For instance, someone belittled as a child might struggle with low self-esteem, while a person who suffered emotional abuse may find it difficult to open up to their partner.

These unresolved wounds manifest in various ways. You may avoid social situations, struggle with decision-making, or experience difficulties in both your personal and professional life. Such patterns are often rooted in the hurt and trauma from your past, and they can create significant obstacles in your journey toward healing and fulfillment.

Yet, by recognizing these patterns and confronting their underlying causes, you can begin to heal. This process involves developing coping strategies and breaking free from the emotional chains that have held you back for so long. The pain of those experiences may linger, but you possess the power to rise above them.

As you examine how your past continues to influence your present, you might uncover lingering patterns of self-doubt or fear. These feelings often stem from how you perceived yourself in your youth—perhaps feeling unloved, unwanted, or rejected. If left unchecked, these feelings can harm your relationships and choices, leading you to sacrifice your happiness and integrity.

Fear can dominate your life if you allow it, preventing you from taking risks or seizing new opportunities. When fear is in control, it often leads to frustration and hopelessness. But you are ready to heal and move forward.

Stop letting past hurts define you. You are stronger than you think. Focus on your strengths, not your weaknesses. Your past does not dictate your future—you have the power to create the life you want.

Negative thoughts rooted in self-doubt can be significant obstacles that hold you back from achieving your goals. When you allow these thoughts to dominate your mindset, you may settle for a life that is less than you deserve because you believe you are not capable of achieving more. But this belief is a harmful lie that can have long-lasting consequences.

Consider the stories of successful individuals like Thomas Edison and J.K. Rowling. Edison faced over 1,000 failures before inventing the light bulb, and Rowling was a single mother on welfare when she wrote the first Harry Potter book.

They could have easily given up on their dreams due to self-doubt, but they chose to believe in themselves, and their perseverance paid off. Similarly, you are capable of far more than you realize.

It's time to stop listening to the inner voice that discourages you and start believing in yourself, your strengths, and your abilities. You deserve a life rich in purpose, passion, and fulfillment, one that unlocks your true potential.

Compromising, especially with children, family, or friends, may seem easier. You might believe that making tough choices will lead to conflict or loss, but settling for less often brings its problems, eroding your self-respect and happiness.

When you compromise your values, you lose touch with who you truly are. It is time to stand up for yourself and live a life that feels authentic to you.

Satan, the enemy of your soul, seeks to amplify your fears and make you doubt your ability to handle life's challenges. Yet, God sees your heart and hears your cries for help. Satan wants you to believe you are not strong enough, but God knows your strength, even when you do not.

Turn to God for guidance, and with His help, you can overcome your fears and live a life that reflects your true self.

As a child of God, washed in the Blood of the Lamb, you have been bought at a price. The Lord paid the ultimate price on the cross, granting you the right to come before His Father's Throne. You can ask for anything according to His will, knowing that you are loved, valued, and capable of greatness.

Through prayer and faith, you can tap into God's strength and receive the courage you need to stand firm in your convictions. Your values shape your identity and guide your decisions. When you stay true to what matters most, you'll experience peace and contentment from being authentic.

2 Corinthians 5:17 reminds us, "If anyone is in Christ, he is a new creature. Old things have passed away; behold, all things have become new."

This transformation is possible because of Jesus' sacrifice on Calvary. Apply the power of His Blood to every area of your life—your mind, thoughts, and deeds. Allow Him to renew your mind daily and keep your focus on Him through prayer.

God will give you the wisdom to make good choices and guide you on the right path. His Word is filled with promises that can strengthen your heart and soul. Memorize these promises and repeat them when you need encouragement.

Embrace His love and let it heal the wounds of your past. Trust in His promises and allow His Spirit to guide you toward a life of joy, peace, and fulfillment.

With God by your side, you can overcome any obstacle and live a victorious life.

Revelation of Truth

Do not call unclean what God has cleansed. Your imperfections are His glory. How you see yourself is not how God sees you. The lies the enemy tells you are not the truth.

The enemy may use even those close to you, like family, to disrupt and discourage you, but God sees their hearts. Keep your eyes on Him, and He will make you a new creation.

Just as the Blood of Christ is redeeming and necessary, so is your bloodline in your family. The blood speaks, carrying memories like DNA cells. God has placed wisdom in your heart to help those who are lost and in need.

Listen to the still, small voice within, and let God guide you to the truth. He will use your voice to set others free and use your mistakes to discipline you, for whom He loves, He chastens.

God's truth will set you free from the enemy's lies. The voice that speaks to your heart is God's voice, guiding you to share His love with others. Your struggles are not a surprise to God. He uses them to shape you into the person He wants you to be.

This process refines your character and strengthens your faith. As you grow, you will become a light to others, showing them the way to freedom and hope.

CHAPTER 8
DO YOU FEEL DIFFERENT?

Do you often feel like an outsider, as if you're stuck on the periphery while others effortlessly connect? Does this nagging sense of being different erect an invisible barrier between you and others, even when you're desperate to belong?

Maybe you've tried to shake off this feeling of being an outcast, but it only seems to get stronger. You're left wondering if there's something wrong with you, or if everyone else is just pretending to have their lives together. This sense of disconnection can be overwhelming, making you feel like you're wandering alone in the dark, searching for a glimmer of hope.

Perhaps you've felt the sting of being ostracized, like a child left out of a game on the playground. It was not your doing, but due to circumstances beyond your control, like being the new kid in town or having a different accent.

Maybe you've always yearned to blend in, to feel accepted and part of a group, like a puzzle piece that finally finds its fit. Yet, it always seemed just out of reach, like a mirage on a hot desert road.

For instance, consider the story of Ruby Bridges, who in 1960 became the first African American student to integrate an all-white school in New Orleans. She faced daily ostracism, with parents pulling their children out of school and protesters chanting outside the building. Despite this, Ruby persevered, and her courage paved the way for future generations.

Ostracism can be a crushing experience, making you feel like an outcast, someone who doesn't belong. It's like being a tree without roots, vulnerable to the whims of the wind. But, like Ruby, you can rise above it, finding strength in your resilience and the support of those who accept you for who you are.

You may have tried to fit in by changing who you are. You may have hidden your true self to avoid rejection. But deep down, you know this isn't the answer. You know that being true to yourself is the key to breaking free from feelings of insignificance and isolation.

Imagine being the new kid in school, walking into a bustling cafeteria where cliques have already formed, and you're not sure where you fit in. You scan the room, searching for a friendly face or a table with an open seat, feeling like an outsider as you awkwardly hover near the periphery.

Or picture yourself as a minority in a community where everyone else seems to share a common language, culture, or background – like being a Spanish speaker in a predominantly English-speaking town, or a Muslim in a community dominated by Christianity.

You may feel like you're constantly trying to translate, not just words, but customs and values, to fit in with the majority. You wonder if you'll ever find your tribe, where you can be yourself without explanation or apology.

Feeling like an outsider can be suffocating. It transforms everyday conversations into a treacherous obstacle course, where one misstep can lead to embarrassment or rejection. You've put on a brave face, pretending that everything is fine, but beneath the surface, you're silently panicking. The uncertainty is like a heavy anchor, weighing you down, making it hard to keep your head above water.

The desire to fit in is a fundamental human need, rooted in our instinct to belong and feel connected to others. It's the reason we seek out like-minded individuals and join clubs, organizations, and communities that align with our interests and values.

We attend social events, gatherings, and meetings, hoping to find our tribe and feel a sense of acceptance. Furthermore, we spend hours scouring social media platforms, meticulously curating our online personas, and craving validation from our virtual connections.

The constant stream of likes, comments, and shares becomes a vital source of self-worth, a fleeting yet addictive high. Yet, for some, this sense of belonging remains an elusive dream, a constant reminder of their social isolation and feelings of inadequacy.

It's as if they're perpetually stuck on the outside, looking in through a window, longingly gazing at the warmth and laughter within. The pain of being an outsider can be crushing, leaving deep emotional scars that linger long after the initial hurt has passed.

But imagine if you could shatter the chains of isolation that bind you. What if you could stumble upon a profound sense of belonging, one that radiates from within? This sense of belonging wouldn't stem from the approval of others, but rather from a rich, unshakeable understanding of your inherent strengths, the passions that fuel your soul, and the values that guide your very existence.

Imagine yourself standing confidently on the podium, baton in hand, ready to lead your unique symphony. Just as a skilled conductor expertly weaves together the diverse sounds of the orchestra, you must intentionally harmonize the various aspects of your life to create a beautiful, authentic whole.

This means recognizing the distinct rhythms and melodies that make up your daily existence - your relationships, work, hobbies, and values - and learning to balance them in a way that resonates with your true self.

As you take the lead, you'll notice discordant notes - areas where your actions and intentions clash - and make deliberate choices to bring them into harmony. The result is rich, soulful music that echoes your deepest desires and aspirations, a symphony that is unmistakably yours.

The path to self-acceptance is long and winding. But it can lead to a rare freedom and power.

It's hard to find them while trying to fit into someone else's mould.

You must prepare to face challenges that test your resolve. These challenges will push you to redefine what you stand for and what you want to achieve. You'll need to sift through the noise of others' opinions and stay true to your vision.

You might have tried to fit in. You attended events, joined groups, and took part in activities. Yet, you still felt like an outsider. This can lead to questioning whether there's something wrong with you or if others are merely pretending to be "normal."

**God's Message to His Children Who Have Felt Like They Never Belonged: **

GOD REASSURES US THAT He has placed us exactly where He wants us, equipping us with unique gifts that reflect His character. These gifts allow us to live according to His plan, free from the constraints of trying to fit into the world's moulds.

By using us as His instruments, God showcases His transformative power to others, just as a master artist uses a brush to create a stunning painting. People may notice a difference in us. They may be drawn to the hope and peace of our relationship with God. It's like a light that attracts ships to a safe harbour.

Consider the remarkable story of the Apostle Paul, a former zealous persecutor of Christians who underwent a profound metamorphosis. Before his conversion, Paul, then known as Saul, was determined to eradicate Christianity, imprisoning and punishing its followers.

However, his life took a drastic turn on the road to Damascus, where a sudden and inexplicable encounter with a blinding light and the voice of Jesus Christ shook him to his core.

This pivotal moment marked the beginning of Paul's transformation into a fervent and formidable advocate for Christ. His radical change of heart inspired countless people to emulate his example, drawn by the sincerity and conviction with which he preached the Gospel.

As a result, Paul's remarkable transformation had a profound impact on the spread of Christianity, igniting a fire that would burn brightly for centuries to come.

When God works through us, our changed lives testify to His power. They inspire others to seek the hope and peace we have found.

Paul's new life took him to cities across the ancient world, where he boldly preached about Jesus Christ. He faced fierce opposition, but his courage and conviction inspired others to stand firm in their faith.

The letters Paul wrote to these early Christian communities still speak to us today, offering guidance and encouragement amid life's challenges. Through his story, we see that God can use anyone, no matter their past, to do great things.

It's as though God has lit a beacon within us, radiating His love and presence, so others may glimpse His glory through our lives.

This message gives us hope—we no longer need to feel like outsiders. Instead, we can embrace our uniqueness, knowing that God created us this way for a purpose.

When we stop hiding who we truly are, others will notice. They will see God's work in us and start asking questions. Love, compassion, and empathy flow from God to His children.

We become channels of God's love, reflecting His character to those around us. As we live out our faith, people will detect the authenticity of our relationship with God.

They will observe how we respond to life's trials, and our reactions will either draw them to God or push them away. Our stories, like Paul's, can inspire others to seek God, too.

In these last days of turmoil, we must manifest the character of Christ, allowing our fervent passion and unwavering zeal to drive His sacred mission forward. As the forces of evil encircle us, squeezing the life out of our communities, the faithful lift their voices in desperation, crying out to God for divine refuge from the crushing weight of injustice.

They yearn for the protective canopy of His mercy, just as the prophets of old sought shelter in the cleft of the rock. Like the apostle Paul, who stood firm against the tumultuous roar of the Roman Empire, we too must stand resolute, our faith unshaken, our hearts afire with a passion that cannot be extinguished.

Free from pretense, we discover our authentic selves through divine love. No longer chasing others' approval or squeezing into ill-fitting moulds, we break free. God's steadfast affection empowers us to shed exhausting facades and embrace who we truly are.

Instead, we can surrender to the life God has crafted for us—a life that radiates purpose and direction. His blueprint isn't for us to get lost in the crowd, but to stand tall as beacons of hope in a world shrouded in darkness.

God's love can illuminate our lives, attracting those who are desperate for His presence like a magnet to metal filings. We become a refuge for the weary, a testament to the transformative power of His love.

We must keep our hands in His, trusting Him to protect us from the enemy's snares. God is the Shepherd who watches over His flock, and if one sheep goes astray, He doesn't forget it but goes after it. The angels in heaven rejoice over one found sheep because God guides His sheep where He wants them to go, and they follow Him.

By living as examples of God's love—through kindness, patience, and humility—we can share what we've learned with others. This isn't about forcing our beliefs on them but being a living example of God's love. When we live authentically, people will see the difference and want to know why.

When we live as examples of God's love, we start a ripple effect of kindness in the world. Our actions inspire others to do the same, creating a chain reaction of compassion.

We don't have to look far to find people who are hungry for God's love. They're all around us, waiting to be touched by His kindness. By being vessels of His love, we open the door for them to experience it too.

We become God's vessels, spreading love, and hope to those around us. By being humble and gentle, we reflect God's character, giving others a glimpse of His goodness.

God has called us, and He will unfailingly stand by our side, never abandoning us in times of need. With His all-seeing eyes, He observes everything, from the smallest detail to the deepest secret, both in the open and hidden from human sight.

Wherever we go, be it busy cities or quiet countryside, God is with us. His constant presence comforts and guides us. In sacred spaces like churches, mosques, or temples, this sense of divine companionship grows.

The air is thick with the prayers and devotion of countless believers. In these holy places, we can almost feel the gentle touch of His hand on our shoulders, reassuring us that we are not alone.

Love from above transforms, not merely touches. Purpose-driven lives spark curiosity. Listen intently and share openly. Through these connections, we embody divine love. Our actions speak louder than words, igniting change and fostering meaningful relationships.

This active demonstration of God's love ripples outward, inspiring others and creating hope for those who have lost their way.

We are a people uniquely chosen by God, separated from the world to fulfill a special purpose. As we draw nearer to Him, His presence becomes increasingly palpable, making us stand out even more. Just as a magnet attracts iron filings, God's Spirit draws us to Himself, setting us apart from those around us.

We are no longer our own; we belong to the Lord, and His Spirit takes up residence within us, guiding and directing our thoughts, words, and actions. This divine ownership is not a distant concept, but a living reality that shapes our daily lives.

As we surrender to His will, we become more distinct, like a beacon shining brightly in the darkness, a testament to God's power and love.

He deliberately positions us in circumstances where we can openly acknowledge His presence. Does this make us stand out in a crowd? Maybe so. However, when we speak of God, our words can inspire hope. They can uplift the grieving and calm the anxious.

Consider the story of Job, who in the face of unimaginable loss, still proclaimed, *"Though he slay me, yet will I hope in him"* (Job 13:15).

His unwavering trust in God brought comfort to those around him. Similarly, when we speak of God, our words can be a balm to the hurting and a beacon of hope in dark times, reminding them that they are not alone.

As we share our stories, we illuminate the dark world around us with God's light. This sets us apart, not in a way that makes us aloof or distant, but as God's children.

We will face challenges when sharing God's love. Some may not want to hear our stories or may mock us. But we must not let fear silence us. God is with us, giving us the right words at the right time.

God's love gives us the courage to stand firm in our faith. This courage helps us speak up when others may not want to listen. We can share our stories boldly, even in the face of opposition.

As we do, we become a source of comfort to those around us. Our words can calm their fears and give them hope for a better tomorrow.

Many walk this earth feeling dead inside, believing that this life is all there is. The enemy has blinded them to the truth, but God sets His light in those He has chosen to free them. God's light shines in us so that we can shine it on others.

We are His ambassadors, spreading love and hope to a world in desperate need. The enemy wants to keep people in darkness, but we can be the light that sets them free. Our stories of God's power and love can revive the hopeless and renew their faith.

We are redeemed by the precious blood of Jesus, the ultimate symbol of His sacrifice for us.

This monumental act of love not only sets us apart but signifies our adoption as His children. Jesus' selfless act on the cross secured for us the gift of eternal life, a promise that echoes throughout eternity.

As the apostle Paul wrote, *"God demonstrates His own love for us in this: While we were still sinners, Christ died for us" (Romans 5:8).* This love transforms us into His beloved children.

God's power changes us from the inside out, making us new people with a new purpose. We are no longer slaves to fear or darkness; we are free to live for God and share His love with others. The enemy may try to silence us, but we will not be quiet. We will tell everyone who will listen about God's love and power.

God's nature is not one of aloofness or distance but is deeply rooted in unconditional love. His love is a powerful force that transforms lives and brings people closer to Him.

History shows this. It is clear in His close relationships with biblical figures like Abraham and Moses. It is also evident in His ultimate sacrifice of Jesus Christ on the cross to redeem humanity.

We are called to reflect God's boundless love toward our neighbours, just as He has lavished it upon us. His love is not fleeting but a powerful catalyst that can alter lives. By serving others, we become instruments of God's love. When we care for the poor, we embody God's love, reminiscent of Jesus' teachings to prioritize the welfare of the most vulnerable.

When we stand up for justice and fairness, we are beacons of God's love, shining brightly in a world often marked by injustice and oppression. By loving our neighbours, we make God's love tangible, lighting up the world and deeply touching those around us.

God's love is unstoppable. It reshapes our lives, conquering challenges and forgiving past mistakes. We know genuine love when we feel it; it's divine and reveals itself through deep spiritual encounters and the selfless acts of others.

God's love stays with us, even in the darkest times, never fading or losing its power. When we face trials, God's love helps us stand strong, like a rock that holds us up.

Love is not just a feeling; it's an action. When we help others, we show them God's love. This can take many forms—visiting the elderly, caring for the sick, teaching those who want to learn. By doing these things, we bring God's love to life, making a difference in the world.

When we serve others, we serve God. This service brings us closer to Him, filling our hearts with joy and giving us a sense of purpose. When we help those in need, we experience God's love firsthand, seeing it in their smiles, gratitude, and hope.

Caring for others helps us feel God's love and connects us to something bigger than ourselves. We see this love when a neighbour sacrifices their time to care for a stranger. Or, when a community rallies around a family that has lost everything. This kind of love reminds us that God is present, working through human hearts to bring hope and healing to a broken world.

When we care for others, we also learn to love ourselves. Helping others shows us that we are capable of making a difference and brings us joy. As we see the impact of our actions, we start to feel more confident and happier with who we are.

CHAPTER 9
ARE YOU SLY?

God's Message to His Clever Children

Have you ever felt proud of your cunning nature, only to have others perceive you as deceitful or untrustworthy? This mismatch between how we see ourselves and how others view us can be a source of frustration and confusion.

As God's children, we must re-examine our motives and methods. Our self-reliance can be seen as sly or dishonest. Instead of relying on our cleverness, we are called to put our trust in God's provision, seeking His guidance and wisdom in times of need.

This requires cultivating patience and perseverance, even when His blessings seem slow in coming. By doing so, we can resist the temptation to take matters into our own hands and instead wait expectantly for God's plans to unfold. Like the Israelites, we must wait for the Lord, trusting that His timing is perfect, even when things seem uncertain.

In our desire to control our lives, we may try to outsmart others to get what we want. But God sees through our tricks. He knows when we're manipulating situations to fit our plans, and He understands that this isn't the path to true happiness.

We might believe our actions are justified, but God sees our hearts and knows when we're acting out of selfish desires. We must recognize when we are trying to manipulate people or circumstances and then confess these wrong motives, seeking God's forgiveness.

Sometimes, our cleverness can backfire, leading to unexpected and often humorous consequences. Have you ever tried to "improve" a recipe by adding your twist, only to end up with an inedible dish? Or perhaps you attempted to outsmart a tough situation, only for your clever solution to worsen things?

These moments remind us that God is always in control. When we try to outsmart others, we're essentially saying we don't trust God to take care of us. This approach can lead to guilt, shame, and fear. Instead, we should seek God's guidance and pause to hear His response. This is the path to true peace and happiness.

Consider the legendary tale of the Trojan Horse. The Greeks, led by Odysseus, devised a cunning plan to infiltrate Troy by hiding warriors inside a massive wooden horse. The Trojans, thinking they had won the war, brought the horse inside their walls, only to be surprised when Greek warriors emerged at night, leading to the downfall of Troy.

Likewise, in daily life, our intelligence can subtly but profoundly fail us. Seeking shortcuts or quick fixes often leads to bigger problems down the line, like a driver taking a shortcut through a busy neighbourhood to avoid traffic, only to end up in a worse jam or lost in an unfamiliar area.

Overthinking can cause us to overlook simple, obvious solutions. It's essential to balance cleverness with common sense, ensuring that our ideas don't backfire and make us look foolish. This often happens when we attempt to solve problems independently, neglecting to seek God's guidance. Trusting in God's ways, not our tricks, leads to wisdom and fulfillment.

God, as our all-knowing Creator, watches over every move we make, and these actions have a lasting impact that extends far beyond our mortal lives. It's easy to get caught up in the pursuit of fleeting triumphs, but we should strive to seek divine wisdom instead.

God's path leads to deep fulfillment that surpasses the temporary highs of worldly success. When we trust in His timing, we're rewarded with an unshaken peace, one that the world's fleeting accomplishments can't begin to touch.

Consider the story of Joseph, who was sold into slavery by his brothers, only to rise to become a powerful leader in Egypt. He trusted in God's plan, even when it didn't make sense, and was ultimately used to save his family from famine.

Similarly, God's plan for our lives unfolds as it should, quietly satisfying our deepest longings, even when we can't see the bigger picture.

When impatience arises, remember that God's plan is beyond our understanding. Like a master artist, He sees the full picture of our lives and knows how to shape it into something beautiful. We must resist the urge to act hastily and instead wait on Him. Trusting in His timing demonstrates our reverence for Him and strengthens our faith.

Like a dedicated farmer who, day and night, tends the land, we too can find peace by surrendering to divine providence. This trust, much like the gentle nurturing of a delicate sapling, allows our souls to flourish with profound contentment.

Just as a gardener's toil yields a great harvest, so too does our faith in a higher power. It brings us a deep, unshakeable peace. As we let go of our need to control, we create space for faith to take root, much like the way a seedling grows strong and tall when tended with love and care.

When we trust in God's provision, we can let go of anxiety about the future, recognizing that He has a plan to meet our needs, even when we are unsure how. This trust brings peace and gratitude, as His timing is always right and purposeful.

God desires to meet the needs and desires of His children. Sometimes, when He says "no," it's because He has something better in store, tailored specifically for us, arriving precisely when we need it.

When obstacles arise, and progress seems to slow, God steps in, weaving our experiences together for our benefit. Even when His timing doesn't make sense to us, trusting in His sovereignty is crucial, especially during life's toughest moments.

Romans 8:28 tells us that "in all things, God works for the good of those who love him, who have been called according to his purpose."

We may not see the good right away, but we can often look back and see how our struggles have strengthened our character, much like a blacksmith who hammers metal to make a strong sword. This reflection helps us trust God more, even in tough times.

When hardships come, it's natural to question why God allows them in our lives. We may wonder, "Where is He hiding?" or "Why isn't He intervening to rescue us?" But God is always at work, even when the darkness seems to overshadow us, and we can't see His hand.

He uses these challenges to shape us, moulding us into the strong, courageous, and compassionate people He wants us to become. Think of it like a master craftsman shaping a rough piece of clay into a beautiful work of art.

This spiritual refinement can be a painful, challenging experience, much like a fiery furnace that melts away impurities, leaving only pure gold. Yet, it is a crucial and transformative stage in our spiritual growth. During these times of intense struggle, we discover our innermost strength, forged in the depths of our souls like molten steel.

On the darkest nights, our fears scream the loudest, but it is then that we learn to cling to God's promise of presence and guidance. In this darkness, we learn that even when we feel alone, God whispers, "I am with you." We are never abandoned, and His promise is a rock on which we can trust.

God shapes us through struggles, turning our weaknesses into strengths. This transformation often happens subtly, without our awareness. He chips away at our flaws, sanding rough edges to reveal a masterpiece of character.

Every struggle peels away layers of self-doubt, revealing a strong foundation of faith. The result is a life reflective of God's own heart, one that overflows with love, kindness, and mercy.

By trusting in His guidance, we can navigate life's ups and downs, even when we feel lost or uncertain. Through faith in Him, we begin to see His plan unfolding, even in the darkest times. In this process, we uncover our true selves, shedding the masks we wear to impress others.

God's fire refines us, burning away impurities, and what remains is authentic, genuine, and strong. Through this transformation, we find our voice, purpose, and passion, emerging as new creations, reborn from the ashes of our past.

When we surrender to God, He reveals Himself in surprising ways. Like a gentle stream that slowly carves its path through rocky terrain, God's presence shapes our lives.

In the stillness, we hear His whispers, guiding us toward hope and restoration. As we journey with God, our relationships transform too.

We learn to love others with the same mercy and kindness He shows us. Our words become gentle, our actions thoughtful, and our hearts compassionate.

In turn, we attract people who value authenticity and honesty. Together, we form a community that lifts each other, rather than tearing each other down.

CHAPTER 10
FACE YOUR MOUNTAIN

Overcoming Obstacles and Conquering Fear

We all have our own personal Everest, towering obstacles that seem insurmountable and fears that paralyze us. These mountains could be a big loss, a broken bond, or painful memories. They might be the haunting voices from our past, echoes that whisper we are not good enough, not worthy enough, and will never be enough.

Perhaps it's the fear of failure, the uncertainty of the future, or the weight of our self-doubt. Whatever your mountain is, it's time to stand at its base, take a deep breath, and face it headon. It's time to acknowledge the fear, feel the pain, and confront the doubts that have held you back for too long.

You may try to run from your mountain, but it will always be there, looming in the distance. It may change shape or size, but it won't disappear on its own. You have a choice: let the mountain define you or define the mountain. God is with you, guiding you every step of the way. He won't remove the mountain, but He will give you the strength to climb it.

As you stand at the base of the mountain, feeling the weight of uncertainty and doubt, remember that the journey to the top begins with a single step. It's a daunting task, one that will push you to your limits and test your resolve, but it's in the arduous climb that you'll uncover the hidden strength within you.

This strength isn't something you're born with, but rather something you develop as you navigate the twists and turns of the path ahead. It's the strength that allows you to persevere through the darkest of nights, to find solace during chaos, and to rise above the doubts that whisper in your ear.

It's the strength that will carry you to the top, where the air is thin, and the view is breathtaking. So, take that first step, no matter how small it may seem, and trust that the journey will reveal the depths of your own inner strength.

Many people find themselves stuck, allowing fear and doubt to hold them back from pursuing their goals. However, it's crucial not to let these feelings discourage you. Identify the obstacles in your path, which may seem like giant boulders blocking your way, and break them down into smaller, manageable tasks that you can tackle one by one.

The voices from your past can be deafening, echoing in your mind like a relentless drumbeat.

They might be loud and convincing, but they do not have the final say in defining your worth. Remember, you are more than the sum of the hurtful words spilled on you or the painful actions inflicted upon you.

You are a unique tapestry woven from the threads of your experiences, strengths, and resilience.

It's time to take a stand and let your authentic voice be heard above the din of negativity. Imagine a lighthouse standing tall against the crashing waves of criticism, its beam of self worth illuminating the path ahead.

Silence those who seek to diminish you, not by shouting back, but by living a life that proves them wrong. Every step you take towards self-acceptance and self-love is a powerful rebuttal to the doubters and naysayers.

By focusing on your strengths, you can leverage them to make your goals feel more attainable and within reach. Think about it: when you're doing something you're truly passionate about, you're more likely to be invested in its outcome. This means you'll be more driven to push through obstacles and roadblocks, even when the going gets tough.

For instance, if you're a skilled writer, you may find that you're more motivated to write a novel because you're doing something you love. Conversely, if you're forcing yourself into a career that doesn't play to your strengths, you may find that your motivation starts to wane.

By recognizing and leveraging your natural talents and abilities, you can unlock a profound sense of direction and motivation that will propel you forward, even when faced with daunting obstacles and adversity.

For instance, consider the story of Malala Yousafzai, the young Pakistani activist who continued to advocate for girls' education despite facing life-threatening opposition. Her unwavering dedication was fueled by her passion for learning and her determination to make a difference.

Similarly, when you focus on your strengths, you'll be more resilient in the face of challenges and better equipped to overcome them. This sense of purpose will also inspire enthusiasm, much like a spark that ignites a fire, driving you to take action and pursue your goals with confidence and persistence.

Many successful people have faced setbacks but didn't let failure define them. Walt Disney was fired from a newspaper for being uncreative, yet he went on to create iconic characters like Mickey Mouse.

J.K. Rowling's *Harry Potter* series was rejected by twelve publishers before becoming a global phenomenon. Thomas Edison faced over 1,000 failed attempts before inventing the light bulb, but his perseverance led to a brighter future.

You have the strength to conquer any obstacle, just like the fearless climbers who conquered Mount Everest. Sir Edmund Hillary and Tenzing Norgay, the first to reach Everest's summit, faced unimaginable challenges, but their determination saw them through. Use their stories to boost your confidence.

When you face a challenge, remember that others have overcome bigger ones. They kept going because they believed in themselves and their goals. You can do the same.

You too can rise above challenges and achieve greatness. Don't be held back by fear or doubt. Instead, focus on your strengths and keep moving forward.

Every step you take gets you closer to your goals. Remember, success often lies just beyond the point where you feel like giving up. So, push through the hard times and stay committed to your dreams.

When faced with a daunting challenge, draw on your internal strength, much like these brave climbers. Your inner resilience can carry you through tough times and help you stay focused on your goals. Every small step forward brings you closer to success. You've already started taking small steps toward your goals.

Now, think about what you want to achieve and write it down. Make your goals specific so you know exactly what you're working toward. Share your goals with a trusted friend or family member to gain support and encouragement.

Fear can be a powerful force; whispering lies that you're not good enough or brave enough. But it's time to break free from fear's grip. Stand up to it, take a deep breath, and walk through the doors of opportunity. Think of times when you overcame obstacles.

Remember how you felt? You can tap into that same feeling again. Believe that you can do it, and you'll start to make progress. Celebrate your small wins along the way – they'll keep you motivated and moving forward.

Take control of your fears by facing them head-on. Identify your fears and push through them. You'll be surprised at how strong you are. Believe in yourself and your abilities. You've made it this far, and you can keep going.

Many individuals stay in their comfort zones, bringing them more misery than joy. They are afraid to explore the unknown, worry about what others might think, and play it safe, hesitant to take risks. This avoidance often culminates in regret, with haunting "what ifs" lingering in their minds.

To break this cycle of fear, you must be brave. Confront your fears, like a daredevil staring danger in the eye. Acknowledge your fears, but don't let them define you.

Embracing your fears will help you grow as a person. You'll learn to accept that fear is natural and it's okay to feel scared. But don't let it stop you from moving forward. Focus on what you want to achieve and let that drive you.

Keep pushing forward, even when it's hard. Fear is normal; everyone faces it. Focus on your strengths and the progress you've made so far. This will give you the confidence to take the next step. Imagine standing at the foot of Mount Everest, weighed down by fear.

The only way to reach the top is to push through the doubt and take the first step. As you do, fear loses its grip, and the path ahead becomes clearer. Each step forward gives you more confidence and sharpens your focus.

Now, picture yourself at the top of Mount Everest. You've made it! The feeling of pride and fulfillment is overwhelming. You look back at the journey, remembering the doubts and fears that tried to hold you back. But you didn't let them win. You pushed through, and it paid off.

For years, fear may have controlled your decisions, but you can break free from its grip when you summon the courage to confront it. Like learning to ride a bike after a tumble, you must face your fears to overcome them.

Consider the story of Nelson Mandela, who spent 27 years in prison for fighting against apartheid in South Africa. Despite brutal treatment, he faced his fears and grew stronger. He used his experiences to fuel his fight for equality and justice.

Facing your fears, you find they are not monsters. They are challenges to overcome with determination. Take a deep breath, square your shoulders, and march straight into the heart of what's been holding you back. The liberation you'll experience on the other side will be worth it, bringing you lasting empowerment and confidence.

Now you're standing on the other side of fear. You've confronted your doubts and emerged stronger. The journey wasn't easy, but you pushed through. You discovered that fear was never the problem—it was your reaction to it. When you faced your fears, you took control. You stopped letting fear hold you back and started living the life you wanted.

Three decades ago, I was part of a small church community that took spiritual growth seriously. The church's focus on discipleship created a safe space, allowing individuals to explore their passions and develop their talents.

Despite this encouragement, I struggled to overcome my fear of singing in front of others. But when I discovered the liberating power of God, I began to express myself through songwriting.

I started small, singing in front of a few trusted friends. Their support boosted my confidence. I took another step and performed in front of a larger group at church. The rush of excitement I felt after facing my fear surprised me. I realized that my fear was not a weakness but an opportunity to grow.

After years of wrestling with my fears, I decided to face them and took a stand for Jesus. I told the enemy that since God gave me this big mouth, I would sing for Him. This decision broke the shackles of fear, and I was free to sing for God.

I still remember the day I decided to take a leap of faith and surrender my life to Jesus. It was a turning point that led to a thrilling adventure. I teamed up with a talented musician and singer, and together we created something amazing – a song that would soon resonate with many hearts.

He titled it "Proud to Be Canadian," a anthem that celebrated our nation's values and spirit. But we didn't stop there. We took our creation to the airwaves, promoting it on the radio for all to hear. It was exhilarating to see how our song brought people together, uniting them in their pride for our country. And it all started with one simple decision: saying yes to Jesus.

I began to share my music with others, performing at local events and gatherings. People appreciated my songwriting, and this feedback strengthened my faith in the liberating power of God. It reminded me that I was not alone in my journey.

My faith gave me the courage to pursue music, and my songs touched people's hearts, helping them through tough times. As I looked out at the crowd, I knew I was making a difference.

I met people from all walks of life, each with their struggles and successes. Their stories inspired me to write more songs—songs that would comfort and uplift. I wrote about hope, perseverance, and the love of God. As I performed, I saw tears of joy, smiles of encouragement, and heads held high.

Embrace your fears boldly and take the first step towards overcoming them. Utilize your unique skills and abilities to make a positive impact on those around you and let your true potential shine through.

As individuals, we have a responsibility to use our gifts to serve others and enhance their lives in meaningful ways. By acting now and seeking spiritual guidance, we can find a fulfilling purpose. Remember, fear is a natural response to the unknown, but how we respond to it defines us.

When we confront our fears, we open ourselves up to new experiences and opportunities for growth. Similarly, using our talents to help others benefits them and brings us a sense of joy and satisfaction. By serving others, we serve ourselves as well.

As we act, it's essential to pray for guidance and seek wisdom. This allows us to move forward with confidence, knowing that we're on the right path. This can create a ripple effect of kindness and compassion, enriching those around us and impacting our communities.

CHAPTER 11
MEMORIES THAT SHATTER

The Impact of Traumatic Memories

Traumatic memories can fracture our souls, leaving behind emotional shrapnel that lingers for years. This is especially true for those who have endured or witnessed violence or trauma, such as soldiers returning from war, abuse victims, and disaster survivors.

These experiences can inflict intense emotional pain, distorting our sense of self and making it difficult to recognize who we once were.

Traumatic memories can also trigger strong physical reactions. Your heart may race, your palms may sweat, and your body may tense up when you recall the event. Sometimes, these memories can cause nightmares, flashbacks, or anxiety attacks, disrupting daily life. God wants to free you from these wounds, but it's a process that takes time and trust.

Our minds, to cope with the crushing weight of traumatic experiences, create new mechanisms to handle the unbearable - much like a computer generating new files to store overwhelming data, preventing a system crash.

This psychological survival strategy, however, comes at a steep cost, such as fragmentation of memories, disconnection from reality, and emotional numbness. For instance, victims of war often develop dissociative identities to shield themselves from the horrors they've witnessed, while those who've experienced childhood abuse may repress traumatic memories, only to have them resurface later in life.

By compartmentalizing our emotions, we may momentarily evade the pain, but ultimately, this coping mechanism can lead to a fractured sense of self and strained relationships.

God's healing process starts with acknowledging the pain we've buried. This means we must face our memories, no matter how painful they are. It's like opening those new files our mind created to store the trauma, but this time, we do it on purpose.

These memories can alter how we react to people and situations, making us feel anxious or stressed even in safe environments. Our bodies may react as if we're still in danger, long after the threat has passed, leading to unexpected feelings of anger, fear, or sadness.

For example, a childhood abuse victim might develop an alter ego as a refuge from the trauma, while a combat veteran might build mental barriers to numb the pain of losing a comrade. These coping mechanisms may help us survive, but they also leave us feeling lost and disconnected from our true selves.

It's like navigating a familiar city with a fragmented map, where roads and landmarks are distorted and unclear, hindering our ability to form healthy relationships, find purpose, and experience joy.

Healing is a journey that starts when we muster the courage to confront the painful experiences that have left us broken.

It's the moment we decide to face our deepest wounds, no matter how agonizing the memories may be. This confrontation is essential because it allows us to process our emotions, which are often tangled in a web of guilt, shame, and anger.

When we finally release the painful memories that have haunted us, we can begin to rebuild and rediscover ourselves. This liberation from the past is a crucial step toward wholeness and recovery, enabling us to move forward with a newfound sense of purpose and direction.

The Mind's Protective Mechanism

In response to trauma, the mind erects a protective barrier to shield us from the full force of our experiences. This defense mechanism, while essential in the short term, can lead to long-term issues, masking our true identities and controlling our lives.

Trauma scatters our sense of self, much like a shattered mirror, leaving behind a trail of jagged shards that pierce our psyche. The fragments of our former self lie scattered, reflecting distorted images of who we used to be. Fear and loss become our constant companions, haunting us like ghosts that refuse to be exorcised.

They lurk in every shadow, echoing the whispers of "what if" and "if only." The mirror's cracks spread; a spider's web of fractures that threatens to consume us whole. Each shard, a painful reminder of the traumatic event, sears our memory like a branding iron.

The broken glass of our self lays bare, a mosaic of past hurts, staring back at us with cold, unforgiving eyes. Every glance forces us to confront the abyss of our own vulnerabilities, leaving us feeling fragile and lost.

Chronic fear can paralyze our growth, making us hypervigilant and constantly on the lookout for threats. This heightened state of alertness causes stress, anxiety, and various health issues, such as headaches, insomnia, and digestive problems. Over time, unrelenting fear wears us down, making it difficult to function normally in our everyday lives.

The Revelation of Truth

The path to healing lies in embracing the truth of God's promises. He assures us that if we walk in His statutes and laws, nothing can harm us. By keeping our eyes on Him, we can navigate life's challenges without being singed by the fire or perishing in the storm.

God has placed His righteousness within us, guiding us from an early age. His still, small voice has protected us, even when we were unaware of His presence. By listening to His voice and following His guidance, we can trust that He will lead us through both the mountaintops and the valleys.

When we reach the mountaintop, God provides rest, just as He has done before. Yet, He also calls us to move further, to cross our mountains and glorify Him. In the valleys—the low points of our lives—we find peace and strength, knowing that our Father will never fail us.

God sees the obstacles in our paths, just as the eagle soars high and sees everything below. He will show us many things from afar, including our enemies being crushed under our feet. As we shake off anger, bitterness, and strife, we must trust that He will take care of us.

Overcoming Fear and Doubt

Fear breeds doubt, blinding us to God's presence, even when He stands before us. However, as we remain in prayer and praise, fear and doubt will fade, replaced by faith. Life's challenges are never easy, but God is always with us. There is joy in the morning, even after a night of mourning. His Spirit offers us the strength to reach out and take what He offers.

God's joy is unlike anything we have ever experienced. It is the joy of love, for He is a God of love. His love is pure and trusting, feeding the soul with life. He cares deeply for us and will guide us through life's darkest paths, shielding us from harm. Amid struggles, we must remember that He is our rock, and His love will lift us when we fall.

A Vision of Heaven

Many believe that life is a burden, devoid of joy, but this bleak outlook does not apply to heaven. In heaven, both delightful and solemn aspects coexist. God's love softens even the hardest times, offering comfort in sorrow.

As we trust Him, He turns our darkness into light and our fear into confidence, guiding us through life's storms to a safe harbor.

In heaven, tears of sadness will dry. Laughter and cheer will replace crying and mourning. God's love will soothe our souls, making us whole again. His gentle care will heal our hurts, and His peace will calm our fears.

Heaven is a place of joy, where angels and children laugh and play without the constraints of time or space. It is a testament to the Father's boundless love and wisdom, where both fun and seriousness coexist, allowing us to enjoy our surroundings while reflecting on life.

Jesus said, *"Suffer the little children to come unto me, for such is the kingdom of heaven."* In heaven, our hearts will be full, and our spirits will soar. We will relive happy memories and create new ones, free from pain and fear. God's presence will fill our hearts with love, and we will experience a peace that never ends.

We will see loved ones who went before us, and they will welcome us home with open arms. In the end, our brokenness is not the final word. Through God's healing, we can become whole again.

We can trust that the shattered pieces of our lives will be mended, and we will be restored to the fullness of life that God intended for us.

Our memories may have shattered us, but they will not define us. In God's hands, we can be made new, with a future full of hope and joy.

CHAPTER 12
THE CONCEPT OF TORN SOULS

The Nature of Torn Souls**

"Torn Souls" is a powerful metaphor that embodies the shattered lives of individuals who have faced profound trauma. Their existence is a maze of fragmented memories, like shattered glass, impossible to reassemble. The scars of their experiences run deep, leaving behind a trail of emotional wreckage.

They wrestle with the remnants of their past, trying to make sense of the chaos that lingers within. The memories, once whole, now lay in shards, refusing to be pieced together, a constant reminder of the pain they've endured.

Their past becomes a puzzle with missing pieces, a constant reminder of the pain they've endured. This fragmentation affects their daily lives, making it difficult to form healthy relationships or find peace, leaving them with a deep sense of sadness, anxiety, and depression.

Trauma disrupts the natural flow of memory, much like a virus corrupts a hard drive, making it hard to access crucial information. Individuals with torn souls often feel like outsiders in their own lives, trying to fit into a world that seems to reject them. This sense of disconnection can lead to unhealthy coping mechanisms, prolonging their suffering.

Many seek answers in therapy, support groups, or self-help resources, but these can only offer limited guidance. The gaps in their memories continue to haunt them, making it challenging to move forward. The healing journey for a torn soul often feels like a wild goose chase, with the missing pieces of the past becoming a source of ongoing torment.

The Impact of Fragmented Memories

FRAGMENTED MEMORIES create significant challenges for individuals with torn souls. These memories resurface unexpectedly, often lacking crucial details, leading to frustration, helplessness, and confusion.

This disruption can affect daily life, making it difficult to form close relationships or navigate everyday tasks. Others may misunderstand their confusion and anxiety, viewing them as unreliable or dishonest, which can lead to feelings of loneliness and rejection.

Psychological conditions like post-traumatic stress disorder (PTSD) can severely disrupt memory, leading to a range of distressing symptoms. For instance, a survivor of a traumatic event may experience vivid and unsettling flashbacks, reliving the horror of the incident as if it were happening all over again.

Moreover, intrusive thoughts can invade their daily life, making it difficult to concentrate or focus on everyday tasks. Nightmares can also occur, further blurring the lines between reality and the traumatic experience.

These symptoms can be debilitating, making it challenging for individuals to move on from the traumatic event and reclaim their sense of security and well-being.

These experiences deepen the disconnection from oneself and reality, making it difficult to rebuild a coherent identity. The struggle to recall events coherently or to assemble a complete picture of the past often results in more questions than answers, fueling anxiety and self-doubt.

The Struggle for Clarity and Guidance

In the quest for clarity, individuals often ignore their intuition, convincing themselves that their minds are playing tricks on them. This internal struggle leads to doubt and confusion, making it difficult to trust one's inner voice. Despite the Spirit's constant presence offering guidance, skepticism and the desire for proof often lead to further emotional turmoil and indecision.

The biblical story of Gideon illustrates this deep-seated desire for validation. Gideon, hesitant to trust without concrete evidence, sought signs from God to confirm his mission. This reflects our struggle to trust the guidance we receive, often leading to frustration when clear signs are absent.

Standing at life's crossroads, individuals may experience anxiety, questioning whether they are making the right choices, which can delay important decisions and exacerbate feelings of uncertainty.

** Revelation of Truth**

God's voice within us is a gentle whisper, calling us to let go of our old identities and embrace the new life He offers. His rivers of living water symbolize rebirth, inviting us to immerse ourselves in His healing presence. This call to renewal is an invitation to surrender our pain, fears, and broken lives to God, trusting in His ability to cleanse and restore us.

The process of facing fear and trauma is daunting but necessary for true liberation. Trauma often gives rise to a hardened, protective persona that shields us from further pain. Confronting our trauma requires meeting this older, protective part of ourselves, understanding it as a vital coping mechanism born of necessity.

Through this acknowledgment, we can begin to unravel the tangled threads of our emotional scars, allowing us to weave a new narrative of strength and resilience.

The Shepherd's Care

Just as a shepherd tends to his flock, Jesus, our Shepherd, seeks out the lost and broken, guiding them back to the path of healing. He knows where to find us, even in the darkest corners of our memories, offering comfort and care as we let go of our pain.

Jesus' care is not merely a gentle whisper but an active force that restores us, binding our wounds and shining light into the dark corners of our lives.

In His loving arms, we discover a sanctuary of healing and restoration, where He gently gathers the shattered fragments of our hearts and tenderly stitches our deepest wounds.

It's a refuge that shields us from the darkness of despair, which can otherwise consume us, leading to daunting thoughts of suicide or, in extreme cases, the tragic act itself.

History has shown us the devastating consequences of such despair, as exemplified by the tragic stories of celebrities like Robin Williams or musicians like Chester Bennington, who struggled with mental health issues.

But under the Shepherd's compassionate care, we regain our sense of purpose and footing, and our lives are revitalized, much like a withered plant that's revitalized by nourishing rain.

Just as *Psalm 23 reminds us, "He leads me beside still waters"* and *"restores my soul,"* we find solace in His presence, which brings peace and tranquility to our troubled minds and hearts.

A Final Revelation of Truth

God extends an invitation:

"Give Me your pain, ridicule, and hard, angry feelings so that you can be free. Come to Me with your burdens, grievances, and shattered lives, and I will take them into Myself. I will cleanse them until they are white as snow, and your remembrance of them will be no more."

In this hallowed sanctuary, where the weary and wounded find shelter, the whispers of broken dreams are silenced, and the echoes of shattered lives are replaced with the gentle whispers of hope.

The Shepherd's soothing presence calms the turbulent storms that rage within, slowly polishing the rough, jagged edges of our pain until they shimmer with a radiant glow.

Like a master artisan, He tenderly reassembles the fragmented shards of our lives, weaving them into a tapestry of redemption, where every thread tells a story of renewal and restoration.

Here, in this sanctuary of solace, we find our bearings, our purpose reborn like a phoenix from the ashes of despair. As we bask in the warm, golden light of His love and guidance, our lives are transformed, resurrected from the darkness of hopelessness, and we emerge, reborn, with a sense of direction and belonging.

CHAPTER 13
THE NATURE OF RAGE

Rage's Nature

Rage can be a deceptive refuge, offering a false sense of control while concealing its devastating effects. It may seem to shield us from trauma, but it leaves destruction in its wake, consuming rational thought, draining energy, and annihilating relationships.

The Toll of Rage

Rage exacts a heavy toll, not just on mental well-being but also on physical health. It can manifest as headaches, stomach issues, and insomnia, weakening the immune system and even shortening one's life.

For instance, a war veteran haunted by battlefield memories might turn to rage as a coping mechanism, offering brief relief but ultimately leading to outbursts that alienate loved ones and dismantle their support network.

Rage often begins with a small grievance, gradually growing into full-blown fury. Initially, it may seem to justify one's anger, but it soon distorts reality and blurs the line between right and wrong. This chaos leads to reckless choices, resulting in shattered relationships and emotional wreckage.

Rage as a Self-Destructive Force

Unchecked rage is toxic, triggering a self-destructive avalanche of behaviors like addiction and self-harm. Like wildfire, it consumes the individual, leaving them isolated, ashamed, and burdened with guilt and regret.

The anger and resentment simmering beneath the surface build into a perfect storm, ending in a complete loss of control. This downward spiral resembles a runaway train, hurtling towards a chaos-filled abyss with severe consequences—fractured relationships, tarnished reputations, and ruined lives.

Lessons from History and Mythology

The ancient Greek myth of the Furies and the writings of Roman philosopher Seneca highlight the dangers of unchecked rage. The Furies tormented those who committed great wrongs, while Seneca warned that "He who does not restrain his anger will be restrained by it." These lessons underscore the importance of managing anger before it consumes us.

Rage is a toxic coping mechanism that often simmers beneath the surface, waiting to boil over at the slightest provocation. While it may provide a momentary release of tension, it ultimately causes more harm than good. **Recognizing and Replacing Rage**

Recognizing rage as a toxic coping mechanism is the first crucial step toward breaking free from its destructive cycle. This awareness illuminates the need to replace rage with healthier ways of coping with pain.

The 1960s civil rights movement serves as a powerful example of how redirecting collective rage and frustration into non-violent resistance can lead to transformative change. Activists channeled their anger into peaceful protest, resulting in landmark laws and a more just society.

To replace rage with healthier coping mechanisms, it's essential to identify the root of the pain—whether it be personal trauma, a sense of injustice, or feelings of powerlessness.

Once the source of the pain is identified, alternative coping methods like mindfulness, communication, and creative expression can be employed to reduce tension and promote healing.

The Aftermath of Rage

When the initial anger subsides, it often reveals underlying emotions like sadness, guilt, and turmoil. Rage acts as a buffer, delaying the confrontation of these deeper feelings.

After a rage filled episode, we are left to grapple with the damage caused, struggling to mend the chaos and restore stability.

Rage as a Catalyst for Chaos

Rage is a powerful, uncontrolled emotion that can escalate minor disputes into intense conflicts, creating a tumultuous atmosphere. It is unpredictable, breeding fear, mistrust, and instability, which further contributes to chaos and broken connections.

Internally, rage creates chaos by overwhelming a person with conflicting emotions, thoughts, and impulses. This internal turmoil can spill over into external circumstances, intensifying the disorder in one's environment, relationships, and within themselves.

Rage as a Response to Chaos

Sometimes, rage arises from chaotic circumstances or a perceived loss of control. When overwhelmed by disorder, a person may resort to rage as a misguided attempt to regain control or vent their frustration.

However, rage typically exacerbates chaos rather than restoring order, making it even harder to address the underlying issues.

Rage can also serve as a mask for deeper emotional pain or past trauma, acting as a defense mechanism to avoid confronting true feelings. However, this only provides temporary relief, as the unresolved emotions continue to fuel rage, creating a vicious cycle.

Breaking the Vicious Cycle of Rage and Chaos

Rage and chaos often feed into each other, creating a vicious cycle where rage breeds chaos, which in turn fuels more rage. This cycle leads to rising disorder and emotional turmoil, with severe consequences for relationships, work environments, and personal well-being.

Recognizing the signs of growing anger and intervening early is crucial in breaking this cycle. Finding the triggers that ignite rage and addressing them through healthier coping mechanisms can prevent the chaos and destruction that typically follow.

Managing Rage

To manage rage effectively, consider the following steps:

1. **Recognize Triggers**: Identify what sparks your anger and understand its underlying causes.

1. **Practice Relaxation Techniques**: Employ deep breathing, meditation, or physical exercise to calm your mind and body before anger escalates.

1. **Seek God's Help**: Spiritual practices can provide the strength to overcome anger and repair the damage it causes. Psalm 51, which shows David's repentance, serves as a guide for seeking forgiveness and healing. Paul's instruction to the Ephesians to replace rage with love and compassion reminds us to build healthier relationships by forgiving as God forgives.

Seeking God's Guidance

Rage obscures our connection with God, creating a barrier between us and His love. True repentance involves seeking His guidance to overcome anger and restore relationships. By focusing on God's love and seeking His forgiveness, we can break the cycle of rage and

embrace healing.

THE STORY OF MOSES losing his chance to enter the Promised Land due to his anger serves as a reminder of the importance of controlling one's temper. Yet, God's love is boundless, offering us a way out of rage and a path towards becoming beacons of hope and kindness.

God's nature is not characterized by rage. By focusing on Him and following His guidance, we can find peace amid anger. Discernment is crucial in managing rage; we must recognize when negative forces influence us and allow the Holy Spirit to guide us away from destructive anger. Seeking God's wisdom and love can transform rage into understanding, leading to a life of peace and compassion.

CHAPTER 14
THE FRAGMENTED SOUL

The Journey of Healing

Healing from trauma is challenging, often requiring the courage to face painful memories. This process is akin to piecing together a puzzle with missing fragments. It can be confusing and frustrating, yet deeply rewarding as the fragmented parts of the soul start to merge, creating a clearer picture of wholeness and peace.

Each fragment represents a part of the soul that has been fractured by trauma, encapsulating a painful memory or experience. As we engage in the healing process, these fragments begin to merge, helping us understand our pain and gradually leading us to peace and wholeness.

Trauma can shatter individuals, leaving them feeling fragmented and disconnected from their own lives. It's as if vital pieces of themselves - their sense of safety, joy, or identity - have been ripped away, leaving behind a gaping void.

This void can manifest as a persistent feeling of incompleteness, a nagging sense that something essential is missing.

Many people struggle to fill this emptiness, searching for a way to reclaim what was lost. For instance, a survivor of a natural disaster might feel a deep sense of vulnerability, as if the safety net of their community has been torn apart.

Others may struggle to find joy in activities they once loved, feeling like a part of their identity has been erased. This sense of loss can be overwhelming, making it difficult for individuals to move forward and rebuild their lives.

Across the world, there is a universal compulsion to collect, a behavior that extends beyond physical objects to include memories, experiences, and even relationships.

The Drive to Collect

People are driven to gather and hold onto things, often without fully understanding why. This behavior includes not only tangible items like vases, coins, and toys but also intangible aspects like knowledge and experiences.

The act of collecting can provide a semblance of control in a chaotic world, creating order and a sense of achievement. It also fosters connections with like-minded individuals, building bonds and a sense of belonging that can be deeply satisfying.

Historically, the drive to collect has been linked to the desire for control and security. Ancient Egyptians buried their pharaohs with treasures to ensure a comfortable afterlife. Today, collectors often claim to preserve culture or history, but their true motive is often rooted in a deeper, unconscious need.

Compulsive collectors, or hoarders, are driven by an intense urge to accumulate. Their collections can range from valuable items like antique furniture and vintage cars to seemingly trivial objects of personal significance.

However, this compulsion can lead to clutter, strained relationships, and harm to one's well-being.

The tragic story of the Collyer brothers, notorious American hoarders, highlights the extreme consequences of excessive hoarding.

Their home, filled with over 100 tons of possessions, ultimately became their tomb, reflecting society's concerns about the dangers of unchecked accumulation.

The Psychological Roots of Hoarding

Experts have long sought to understand the psychology behind hoarding. Some theories suggest that it is linked to emotional trauma or a need for control in an unpredictable world. However, the root causes are complex and multifaceted.

Hoarders often feel deprived, lacking necessities or emotional security. This drives their compulsion to collect and cling to possessions, many of which hold deep sentimental value.

In a similar vein, people often hold on to relationships or memories that are harmful or misaligned with their values. These toxic connections can hinder personal growth and block the path to happiness.

Letting go of such ties is essential to invite positive influences into our lives, which can help us grow and achieve our goals.

The act of holding onto something—whether it's a possession, a memory, or a relationship— often stems from fear. The fear of losing control, of being without, or of facing the unknown can lead to an intense desire to hold on tightly.

Yet, this grasping can cause deep emotional pain, much like holding onto a hot stove—it inevitably burns.

Revelation of Truth

"Ask what you will, and I will give it to you. I own the vineyard, and all the fruit is mine. Pick the best, and I will turn it into the finished product."

"You have not because you ask not, or you ask amiss. I will give you that which you need, that which will enrich your spirit for My Kingdom."

"First the spiritual, then the natural; as it is in heaven, so shall it be on earth."

*"I am your Heavenly Father, and it is My good pleasure to give to My children the desires of their hearts. I will not withhold anything from those who seek My face.

I long for you to spend more time in My Presence. I supply your needs, not necessarily your wants, according to My Will."*

Many have been conditioned to believe negative things about themselves, such as being slow, incapable, or unworthy. These beliefs, reinforced over time by others and internalized, shape how we perceive ourselves and how we act.

Believing these negative views can lead us to act in ways that reinforce them, creating a cycle of self-sabotage and low self-esteem.

For example, if someone is constantly belittled by a partner, their self-worth may erode over time, leading to a spiral of self-doubt. This toxic environment makes it even more challenging to break free from negative self-images.

However, change is possible. Think of it like a puzzle: when we recognize how our beliefs shape our actions, we can start to rearrange the pieces to form a new picture. This new perspective can help us break free from negative self-talk and limiting behaviors.

When negative beliefs are deeply ingrained, parts of us may fragment or separate from our soul as a defense mechanism. These fragmented parts often try to hide the hurt and pain, but God provides a way out.

"No temptation has overtaken you except such as is common to man; but God is faithful, who will not allow you to be tempted beyond what you are able, but with the temptation will also make the way of escape, that you may be able to bear it." (1 Corinthians 10:13)

If we turn to God now, He will show us that He has been with us all along, sharing in our pain, and waiting for us to reach out to Him. He is ready to reveal Himself to us, but many who suffer are too hurt or ashamed to seek Him.

Yet, He waits in the light, ready to take our hand and lead us out of the darkness.

God hears our whispers in the dark and sees our tears when no one else does. When we feel utterly alone, He is there, ready to take away the shadows that haunt us. We just need to let Him in.

The Role of the Holy Spirit

When we're overwhelmed, it feels as if our souls are shattering into countless pieces. In these moments, we must call upon the Holy Spirit to intervene. The Spirit acts as a master puzzle solver, searching every dimension to find the lost fragments of our souls.

As these fragments are gathered, God reassembles them, declaring, "I am making you whole, a new creation in Me." This process is like a potter reshaping a broken vase, making it stronger and more beautiful than before.

As we heal, we begin to see God's hand in our lives, even during times when we feel abandoned. We come to understand how He used our struggles to strengthen and teach us, revealing that He was always present, even in our darkest moments.

Surrendering to God's Care

SOMETIMES, WE CLING to aspects of our lives that cause us pain—memories, harmful habits, or deep-seated fears. These parts resist change, refusing to surrender to God's healing power. They feel safer in the familiar darkness, even though it harms us.

But the Lord gently calls out to these wayward parts of our souls. As the Good Shepherd, He watches over us, guiding us back to wholeness. Just as a shepherd gathers lost sheep,

God longs to gather the broken parts of our lives, comforting us with His gentle voice and reminding us that we belong to Him. By trusting in His guidance, we can find rest and healing.

Though we may struggle to let go of these parts, clinging to them only brings more pain. They whisper lies that we are unworthy of God's love or too broken to be healed.

But God's voice is louder, reminding us that He loves us as we are, brokenness and all. As we listen to Him, we can release our grip on the past and allow His healing to begin.

Revelation of Truth

Let Jesus speak to those hidden, fragmented parts of your soul:

"You are part of my flock. Some shattered parts are larger because they have been separated for a long time. The longer they have been apart, the more they have grown until they were reasoned with. Smaller parts resist and want to remain hidden and small."

"These smaller, ambling parts have just broken away and are hiding in stiff, sore places. But they are ready to leave their hidden safety net. Other parts, often seen in a meadow, are ready to be called out and are glad to be found."

We need to pray. We must cleanse these fragmented parts in the Blood of Jesus and pray for them to be united into one healthy, whole soul.

Jesus says, *"I am the way, the truth, and the life. He that comes to me shall never hunger, thirst, or be lost."*

CHAPTER 15

FINDING HEALING IN A SAFE PLACE

Why a Safe Place Matters

A safe place is like an anchor in a storm, providing the stability needed to weather life's turbulent moments. It serves as a sanctuary where you can shed the masks worn in the outside world and be your authentic self, free from the fear of judgment or rejection.

In this space, you can finally let your guard down, releasing the tension that has built up inside. This release is the first step in the healing process, where you begin to peel back the layers of emotional scars and rediscover the strength within.

Imagine a secluded sanctuary, surrounded by nature's soothing embrace, where the air is crisp and clean, and the sounds are a gentle hum of serenity. This is your refuge—a haven where the weight of the world, with all its burdens and worries, slowly lifts from your shoulders.

Here, your mind finds calm, like a still pond on a windless day, and you can breathe deeply, feeling the tension and anxiety melt away. Healing begins in this safe space, where you're wrapped in a sense of security and support, like a comforting blanket on a chilly night.

In this serene refuge, the weight of others' opinions lifts, liberating you to reveal your most intimate thoughts, emotions, and deepest fears. This sanctuary offers a peaceful haven, insulated from the daily stress and anxiety that can overwhelm.

It's a place where you can confront the darkest recesses of your psyche, free from the terror of being consumed by your inner demons. Imagine sitting by a still ocean, the soft lapping of the waves against the shore a soothing balm to your frazzled nerves, as you slowly unravel the tangled threads of your mind.

This environment quiets your mind, allowing you to focus on your thoughts and emotions. With each breath, you begin to shed the burdens that weigh you down, and your true self starts to emerge. This space becomes a mirror, reflecting your strengths and weaknesses, leading to acceptance and peace.

As your true self surfaces, the mist shrouding your vision lifts, revealing a path forward. This newfound awareness gives you the courage to let go of the past, embracing the present with open arms. In this state of clarity, you can envision a brighter future, one where you are free to pursue your dreams and desires.

This sanctuary is essential for the healing process, acting as a balm to the soul. It nurtures your vulnerabilities, allowing you to confront and overcome past wounds. It's like finding shelter from a storm, where you can regroup and rediscover your true self.

Having such a place is essential for beginning the challenging but transformative journey of healing and self-discovery. It gives you the courage to face your pain and touch the scars you've hidden from the world.

Embracing Your True Self

Feelings of unworthiness or inadequacy often arise, but they don't define you. Your worth isn't determined by life's challenges but by how you face them. Recognize your resilience and embrace your potential.

By embracing your true self, you open the door to new possibilities. Challenges become opportunities for growth rather than threats. This shift in perspective allows you to find meaning in your struggles, emerging stronger and wiser. In this way, your imperfections become sources of strength, not weakness.

Your true self is a work of art in progress, shaped by your experiences, refined by your struggles, and polished by your strengths. As you embrace it, you'll find that your flaws and scars become an integral part of your beauty. They add depth, character, and uniqueness to who you are.

You may have tried to escape your emotions by blaming others or yourself, but guilt and shame persist. It's natural to wonder why you weren't shielded from harm or taught self-love. However, holding onto these feelings won't change the past. Instead, focus on healing and growth.

Healing and growth start with accepting your story. Your journey, though imperfect, is yours alone. By claiming it, you'll begin to let go of guilt and shame. This freedom allows you to focus on the present, where you can make a difference.

Healing is a journey, not a destination—a path that unfolds over time, marked by twists and turns that shape us into stronger, wiser individuals. Small steps today, like droplets of water, can collect to form a mighty ocean of transformation, leading to significant changes tomorrow.

Start by recognizing your emotions, acknowledging the complex mix of feelings that swirl inside you, and accepting them as valid—not trying to suppress, deny, or numb them. This simple act of self-acknowledgment can bring comfort and peace, much like a gentle breeze on a summer's day, soothing the scars of yesterday.

Although you can't change past events, you can shape a brighter future through self-awareness and forgiveness. Forgiveness helps you release grudges, and resilience allows you to recover.

As you start this journey, you'll begin to rewrite your life story, shedding the weight of past traumas.

Forgiving yourself or others can be difficult but remember that forgiveness is a process. It takes time, effort, and patience. Begin with small steps, and gradually work toward the bigger ones. With each step, you'll feel a weightlifting off your shoulders and start seeing your capacity for change and growth.

REVELATION OF TRUTH

You are a child of the King, set free from past transgressions by the work completed on the cross. Christ's sacrifice has freed you. His light shines upon you, and those whom the Son sets free are truly free.

The enemy tries to make you feel guilty for events beyond your control, but God uses these experiences to help you reach and heal others. What was meant for evil, God can turn into good. Jesus is the Life, the Way, and the Truth.

God allows trials to help you connect with others and guide them toward healing. Despite the enemy's tricks, the Lord transforms your struggles into lessons and healing opportunities. When faced with trauma, parts of us can separate, leaving us with coping mechanisms for crises.

God's purpose is not to leave you stuck in pain. He wants to use your story to help others heal. By facing your trauma, you can find purpose and meaning. Your struggles can become a bridge to connect with others who are hurting.

Let the Holy Spirit help reveal and heal these hidden parts of yourself. Fear can keep you

hidden from healing, but addressing these fears is vital for recovery. The Holy Spirit guides you through the process, making you more aware of god's presence. He wants to use your story to bring hope and healing to others.

CHAPTER 16
HOW TO OVERCOME DEPRESSION AND START A NEW LIFE

Overcoming depression is a significant challenge, one that many of us face in silence. Depression is more than just feeling sad—it's a deep, persistent sense of despair that can rob us of joy, energy, and the will to keep going.

It often creeps in when the weight of unfulfilled desires, regrets, and fears becomes unbearable, leaving us feeling stuck and hopeless.

Depression can make even the simplest tasks seem overwhelming. It can feel like you're trapped in a never-ending cycle of darkness, where getting out of bed feels like an impossible feat. If these feelings last for more than two weeks, it might be time to acknowledge that depression has taken hold.

Identifying Triggers and Seeking Help

The first step towards healing is identifying what triggers your depression. Is it unresolved trauma, the pain of a broken relationship, or the disappointment of unachieved dreams? Recognizing these triggers is crucial because it allows you to confront the root causes of your suffering.

This is not an easy process, but it's a vital one, as it marks the beginning of your journey out of the darkness.

If you're struggling to shake these feelings, seeking medical help is essential. A doctor or therapist can provide you with the tools and support you need to manage your symptoms and work towards recovery.

Depression doesn't just affect your mental state—it impacts your physical, emotional, and spiritual well-being, making professional guidance crucial.

Understanding Depression's Impact

DEPRESSION CAN LEAD to significant changes in appetite, sleep patterns, and energy levels. It can strain your relationships, make you feel guilty or anxious, and numb your emotions. Spiritually, depression may cause you to question your purpose, values, and beliefs, further deepening your distress.

Research has shown that depression affects the brain's structure, particularly the prefrontal cortex, which regulates emotions and motivation. Understanding this helps us see depression not just as a mental state, but as a physical illness that requires attention and care.

Building Structure and Acting

ONE OF THE MOST EFFECTIVE ways to combat depression is to establish a daily routine. This provides a sense of stability and control, helping you stay organized and focused.

If your job is unfulfilling, and you yearn for something more, start by setting realistic goals.

Break them down into smaller, manageable tasks, and create a timeline for accomplishment.

Taking steps toward your dreams, no matter how small, can be empowering. Research the skills you need for your desired career and start building them. Networking, taking courses, or volunteering in your field can all be steps toward a more fulfilling life.

Remember, letting fear dictate your choices can lead to stagnation and deeper depression. By taking proactive steps, you not only build confidence but also open doors to new opportunities and a brighter future.

Overcoming Spiritual Battles

DEPRESSION ISN'T JUST a physical or mental struggle—it's also a spiritual battle. Satan, the enemy of our souls, seeks to keep us trapped in despair, separating us from God's love and purpose for our lives. His tactics—lies, fear, and guilt—can cause us to feel hopeless and disconnected from God.

However, we have the power to resist these lies. When we structure our lives according to God's plan and invite Him to take control, we become His children, heirs to a legacy of spiritual blessings. This gives us the strength to reject feelings of worthlessness and embrace the truth of God's love and promises.

Finding Strength in Faith

Faith is a powerful ally in the battle against depression. Trusting in God provides hope and resilience, even in the darkest times. When life feels overwhelming, turning to God can offer comfort and guidance.

Through prayer, meditation, and other spiritual practices, we can reconnect with our Creator and find the strength to move forward.

Knowing that you are part of a larger community of believers who understand your struggles can be comforting. It reminds you that there is a greater purpose unfolding in your life, even when the path ahead seems uncertain.

Faith acts as an anchor in the storms of life, guiding you toward a future filled with hope, purpose, and fulfillment. Consider the story of Nelson Mandela, who endured years of hardship by holding onto his faith.

Like him, your faith can sustain you, providing a light that leads you out of the darkness and into a new, brighter chapter of your life.

Our spiritual battles and our faith is needed to overcome depression. Overcoming depression is a holistic journey that involves the mind, body and spirit.

CHAPTER 17
OUR ROLES OF MOTHERHOOD

Reflections on Parenting and Free Will The Perception of Failure in Motherhood

As mothers, we frequently engage in self-criticism, magnifying our perceived shortcomings and dwelling on the "what ifs." We may excessively worry that we haven't dedicated sufficient time, provided adequate guidance, or made the right decisions for our children's well-being, education, and emotional development.

This relentless self-scrutiny can lead to feelings of guilt, anxiety, and inadequacy, ultimately affecting our confidence and ability to make decisions.

For instance, a mother may constantly question her decision to return to work, fearing that it might negatively impact her child's cognitive development or emotional security.

Another mother may feel guilty about not being able to breastfeed, thinking that it will hinder her child's health and bonding experience. By acknowledging and addressing these insecurities, we can begin to break free from the cycle of self-doubt and cultivate a more positive, supportive environment for ourselves and our children.

Our children observe us intently, taking in every expression, every reaction. They learn from the way we respond to challenges, whether we face them with courage or crumble under pressure.

When we stumble, they watch closely to see how we pick ourselves up and dust ourselves off. This is why it's crucial that we show them that mistakes are not failures, but opportunities for growth and learning.

We can do this by owning up to our errors, apologizing when necessary, and explaining how we plan to do things differently next time.

By doing so, we teach them the valuable lesson that it's okay to make mistakes, and that it's how we respond to them that truly matters. We can illustrate this point by sharing stories of famous inventors, like Thomas Edison, who famously said, "I have not failed. I've just found 10,000 ways that won't work."

This mindset helps our children grasp a crucial concept: mistakes are stepping stones to success, rather than obstacles to be feared.

When kids understand that errors are an inevitable and essential part of the learning process, they're more likely to embrace challenges and boldly venture into uncharted territories.

They'll begin to see that every mistake provides an opportunity to learn, adjust, and improve, much like Thomas Edison, who famously said, "I have not failed. I've just found 10,000 ways that won't work."

By adopting this mindset, our children will develop a growth mindset, where they view failures as opportunities for growth, rather than threats to their ego.

As a result, they'll be more willing to take risks, think creatively, and push beyond their comfort zones, ultimately becoming more confident, resilient, and successful individuals.

Our children see us in a different light, one that shines brighter than our self-doubt and criticism.

They notice how we've persevered through life's challenges, demonstrating a love that is unwavering, unrelenting, and unshakeable.

They recall the warmth of our hugs, the comforting tone of our voice, and the countless times we've wiped away their tears. They remember how we stayed up late helping with homework, attended every school play and sports game, and celebrated their every achievement, no matter how small.

In their eyes, we are heroes, not because we're perfect, but because we've shown them that love can conquer even the toughest of times.

They learn from our strengths, not just our weaknesses. We model a growth mindset when we try new things, make mistakes, and keep going.

Our children see that it's okay to not know something at first, but it's not okay to give up.

God's boundless love and profound understanding transcend the flaws and shortcomings that often consume us, peering beyond the surface to reveal the authentic and empathetic core that lies at the heart of every individual.

This inherent goodness, much like a beacon of light, shines brightly despite our human frailties, reminding us that we are more than the sum of our imperfections.

In essence, God's love sees the real us, the us that is often hidden beneath the layers of self doubt, fear, and anxiety.

This inherent spirit, refined and fortified through the multifaceted challenges and triumphs of motherhood, is a testament to our capacities.

When we gaze at ourselves through the eyes of our children, who love and admire us unconditionally, it can trigger a profound shift in perspective.

Suddenly, our critical inner voices that focus on our shortcomings begin to quiet, and we start to appreciate the earnest efforts we make every day to provide, nurture, and guide our little ones.

Through this shift in perspective, we start to see ourselves in a new light, as capable, selfless, and strong individuals who make a meaningful difference in the lives of our children.

As we let go of our flaws and shortcomings, we begin to recognize our own value and worth, freed from the grip of self-doubt and negativity.

This newfound self-awareness empowers us to be more patient, kind, and compassionate towards ourselves, just as we are towards our children.

This newfound awareness empowers us to silence our inner critics and celebrate our achievements. We begin to recognize ourselves as strong, capable, and deserving mothers.

By doing so, we set a powerful example for our children, teaching them to embrace their own strengths and weaknesses with confidence.

We must embrace our strengths, recognizing that the resilience and determination we show each day are the very qualities that make us successful mothers.

We stop dwelling on past mistakes and focus on the present moment, where we can make a positive impact on our children's lives. By doing so, we become more confident in our abilities, making better choices that benefit our families.

This confidence boost also helps us to be more open with our children, sharing our own struggles and weaknesses to show them that everyone makes mistakes.

Reflecting on Our Journey

Motherhood is a journey filled with decisions made with our children's best interests at heart, even though some choices might later seem less than ideal. Reflecting on our journey shows our milestones and growth.

We learn to let go of self-doubt and celebrate our triumphs, no matter how small they may seem. This reflection helps us identify areas where we've improved and grown, giving us a sense of pride and accomplishment.

By acknowledging our progress, we're better equipped to make intentional choices that support our personal growth and our children's well-being.

We should celebrate our successes, whether it's raising confident and respectful children, creating a stable home environment, or teaching important life skills. These accomplishments provide a deep sense of purpose and fulfillment.

Our efforts in raising our children contribute to their development into kind, empathetic, and wise individuals. These traits shape our children's future and positively impact the world. By focusing on these values, we enrich our parenting and make a lasting difference in our children's lives.

Accepting Free Will

As parents, our primary responsibility is to establish a strong foundation, offering guidance and support while respecting our children's autonomy to make their own decisions. It's natural to feel anxious when they deviate from our guidance, fearing they may encounter obstacles or make mistakes. However, we must remember that their free will is essential to their growth.

By embracing our children's choices, we discover a profound sense of peace as parents. When their decisions diverge from our expectations, instead of resistance, we opt for acceptance.

This acceptance fosters an unwavering trust in their capacity to grow and learn from their experiences, whether they culminate in triumph or defeat.

Think of it like a tree weathering a storm; its roots grow stronger as it adapts to the turbulent winds. Similarly, our children's ability to navigate life's challenges is fortified as they face and overcome obstacles, shaping them into resilient and self-assured individuals.

As our children exercise their free will, they build problem-solving skills and learn to take responsibility for their actions. This, in turn, helps them develop a strong sense of self, separate from our own opinions and biases.

By giving them space to make mistakes, we empower them to find their own solutions and grow from their experiences.

For instance, when a child chooses a college major that doesn't align with our vision, it can be tempting to intervene and steer them toward a more "practical" path. However, by accepting their decision, we demonstrate faith in their judgment and allow them to take ownership of their educational journey.

As they navigate the consequences of their choices, they'll develop essential skills like problem-solving, critical thinking, and adaptability.

This acceptance doesn't mean we abandon our role as guides; rather, it means we shift from dictating their path to supporting their exploration. By doing so, we create an environment where our children feel empowered to make decisions, learn from their mistakes, and develop a sense of agency that will serve them well throughout their lives.

Our role as mothers is not to control every step our children take, but to offer guidance that empowers them to make their own decisions. By instilling strong values in them, we can trust that they will develop the resilience and wisdom to navigate life's obstacles, from the mundane to the extraordinary.

Remember, a fundamental aspect of motherhood is having faith in our children's capacity to learn from their mistakes, adapt to new situations, and ultimately forge their own paths. By doing so, we not only nurture their independence but also create a strong bond built on mutual trust and respect.

Trusting in Divine Guidance

Scripture advises us to seek God's kingdom and righteousness first. By aligning with His guidance, we can find purpose and trust in the path we've set for our children. We are not responsible for their choices but must provide them with the tools and values they need to make informed decisions. By entrusting our children to God's purpose and letting go, we find calm.

When we place our faith in God's guidance, we can release the grip of fear and anxiety, freeing ourselves to be a calming and reliable presence in our children's lives.

Just as a ship drops anchor in a storm, we can anchor our families in times of turmoil, providing a sense of security and stability.

This allows our children to venture out, exploring their capabilities and limitations, and discovering their passions and interests without the weight of our fears holding them back.

As they navigate life's challenges, they develop a strong sense of self and direction, much like a tree grows deep roots in fertile soil.

By doing so, they become more resilient, better equipped to handle the ups and downs of life, and more confident in their ability to make decisions and chart their own course.

The Role of Free Will and Learning from Mistakes

As parents, we play a significant role in shaping our children's lives by making crucial decisions that influence their futures. We do this with the best of intentions, hoping to guide them onto a path that leads to happiness and success.

When we look back on our parenting journey, we may acknowledge that some of the decisions we made, although driven by good intentions, ultimately didn't yield the desired outcomes. For instance, we might recall a time when we restricted our child's screen time too severely, only to find that it led to more conflict than cooperation.

Or perhaps we encouraged them to pursue a particular hobby, only to discover it wasn't their true passion. These kinds of flawed decisions, made with our children's well-being at heart, can ultimately serve as valuable opportunities for growth, both for our children and for us as parents.

By reflecting on what went wrong and why, we can learn from our mistakes, adjust our approach, and become more effective and adaptable caregivers.

When we recognize a mistake, it's essential to reflect, correct, and try again. This helps us grow and sets a powerful example for our children. They learn that it's okay to make mistakes as long as we take responsibility and strive to make amends. This teaches them the value of humility, accountability, and perseverance.

Building a Strong Foundation and Positive Example

As parents, we should focus on our achievements and blessings. Success isn't about wealth; it's about the values and morals we instill in our children. These treasures endure and guide their descendants through life.

Let's give our children a strong moral foundation that will guide them in this life and the next.

By focusing on our strengths and modelling positive behaviour, we demonstrate to our children how to navigate life's challenges with confidence and resilience.

In difficult situations, choosing patience and understanding over anger teaches our children that they, too, can be strong and wise in the face of adversity.

Consistently showing kindness, honesty, and respect towards others instills in our children the value of empathy and compassion—qualities essential in building strong, healthy relationships and contributing positively to the world.

The Influence of Small Actions

Even small actions can have a big impact. Teaching our children to say "please" and "thank you" or encouraging them to help a friend in need can shape their character and inspire them to grow into compassionate and responsible individuals.

By being mindful of our actions and their impact on our children, we can shape the next generation of leaders who will bring about transformative change. For instance, when we model empathy, our children learn to put themselves in others' shoes and understand their struggles.

They develop a sense of responsibility, recognizing that their actions affect not only their own lives but also the lives of those around them. This empathy can foster courageous leaders who will stand up for what is right, even in the face of adversity. Consider Malala Yousafzai, the young Pakistani activist who bravely defied the Taliban's ban on girls' education.

Her courage has inspired millions of people worldwide to fight for the right to education. By emulating such courageous leaders, our children can grow up to become beacons of hope, driving positive change in their communities and beyond.

Letting Go and Trusting God

As parents, it can be a painful and difficult experience to accept when our children choose a different path in life, one that diverges from the dreams and aspirations we had envisioned for them. We may feel a deep sense of failure, as if we have somehow fallen short in our role as guardians and mentors.

We may also experience a profound sense of loss, mourning the loss of the relationship we had imagined would unfold between us and our child. However, we must remind ourselves that it is their choice, not ours, and that their destiny is not dependent on our approval or validation.

We have invested time, effort, and love into providing them with a strong foundation, instilling in them the values and principles that will guide them through life's journey. Now, we must trust that a higher power, such as God, will continue to guide them, even when their path takes a turn we did not anticipate.

Our role as parents is not to dictate every step our children take, but to model a life that genuinely honours God. By living out our faith authentically, we create a powerful example for our kids, demonstrating that even when life gets uncertain, we can confidently rely on God's guidance.

Think of it like a trust fall – we're showing our children that we trust God to catch them, even when we can't see what's ahead.

We must release our grip on control and trust that our children are securely held in God's hands, just as the psalmist David wrote, *'You hold my right hand' (Psalm 73:23).*

By giving up control, we grant our children the liberty to navigate their own journey, experimenting with decisions and learning from the outcomes.

This can be a daunting but vital step in their development, as it allows them to discover their own strengths and weaknesses.

We must have faith that the moral compass we've instilled in them will steer them towards wise choices. When we do, we demonstrate to our children that we have confidence in their capabilities and trust their judgment.

This, in turn, fosters a sense of self-reliance and empowerment, as they realize that their decisions have real-world consequences.

CHAPTER 18
NO OTHER WAY TO HEAVEN

THE ONLY WAY TO HEAVEN

Jesus declared, "No one comes to the Father except through me" (John 14:6). This statement emphasizes that faith in Jesus Christ as Savior and Lord is the sole path to heaven. Jesus, as the only begotten Son of God, sacrificed His life to offer humanity a place in heaven. Through Him alone, we can connect with God and secure eternal life.

Key Scriptures

John 1:1, 14: "In the beginning was the Word, and the Word was with God, and the Word was God. The Word became flesh and dwelt among us, full of grace and truth."*

This passage underscores Jesus's divinity and His incarnation as a human being. It highlights His unique role in the plan of salvation, being both fully God and fully man.

John 3:16: "For God so loved the world that He gave His only begotten Son, that whoever believes in Him should not perish but have everlasting life."*

This verse underscores the depth of God's love and the centrality of belief in Jesus for eternal life. God's love is the foundation of our salvation. It is through Jesus that God offers us eternal life, not just for a select few but for all who believe.

Ephesians 2:5-8: *"Even when we were dead in sins, He made us alive together with Christ, by grace you are saved. For by grace are ye saved through faith; and that not of yourselves: it is the gift of God."*

These verses remind us that salvation is a gift of grace, not something earned by human effort, but granted through faith in Christ. Our new identity in Christ unites us with God and with one another, forming a community of believers bound by grace.

Salvation Explained

Salvation is the profound process of being rescued from the grip of sin, which would otherwise lead to eternal separation from God. This divine rescue operation is made possible solely through the selfless sacrifice of Jesus Christ on the cross, where He bore the weight of humanity's sins.

By placing our trust in Jesus and His sacrificial love, we receive the gift of forgiveness, wiping clean the slate of our past mistakes and freeing us from the guilt and shame that once bound us. Furthermore, we are granted a new spiritual life, filled with purpose and meaning, as the Holy Spirit takes residence within us.

This new life is not just a one-time event but a lifelong process. As we grow in faith, we see the world through God's eyes, gaining hope and healing that restores our relationships with others and ourselves. Salvation is a gift we could never earn, given freely out of God's boundless love and mercy.

The Sinner's Prayer

For those who genuinely desire to invite Jesus into their lives as their personal Savior, a sincere and heartfelt prayer of repentance and faith marks a crucial initial step in their spiritual journey. This prayer serves as a powerful expression of commitment, signaling a willingness to trust in Jesus for eternal salvation

and redemption.

"GOD, I KNOW THAT I am a sinner. I deserve the consequences of my sin, but I am trusting in Jesus Christ as my Savior. His death and resurrection paid the price for my forgiveness. I trust in Jesus as my personal Lord and Savior. Thank you, Lord, for saving and forgiving me. Amen!"

Assurance of Salvation

The Bible offers strong assurance that salvation is secure for those who place their faith in Jesus Christ.

In Acts 16:31, *Paul and Silas told a jailer, "Believe in the Lord Jesus Christ, and you will be saved."*

This promise remains true today; salvation is offered to all who believe, and it is through faith in Jesus alone that we are assured of a place in heaven.

Salvation is not earned by our efforts or good deeds. As *Ephesians 2:8-9 states, "For it is by grace you have been saved, through faith – and this is not from yourselves, it is the gift of God – not by works, so that no one can boast."*

This emphasizes that our salvation is a gift from God, based on His grace and not on our actions.

We can live with confidence knowing our place in heaven is secure. This assurance allows us to focus on loving and serving others without the fear of losing our salvation.

Romans 8:38-39 reassures us that nothing in all creation can separate us from the love of God that is in Christ Jesus our Lord.

This unshakable confidence in God's love frees us from the burden of performance, allowing us to live joyfully in His grace.

My Personal Testimony

I accepted the Lord in my heart when I was eighteen years old. At that time, I was living in Detroit with my oldest daughter's father. My brother had gotten saved in a little church front in Scarborough. One night he told me later that he and the Pastor of the church, and six others got together and prayed for me to come home to Toronto.

I did not know that he had done this as I was not in touch with my family at this time. I remember feeling a drawing to leave this violent man that I was living with and head for home. All I had were the clothes on my back and my dog. I went over to my sister's at the time and told her I was going home.

She asked me to wait two days, and she could give me bus fare, but I told her I could not wait I had to go immediately. She drove me to the Canadian border, and I hitched a ride all the way to Toronto from Windsor and reached Toronto with just the clothes on my back and my dog, Caesar.

I met a friend of my brother's as I approached my brother's house. He told me about the meetings at the church that night and why don't I come. And so, I went to the little church who had prayed so mightily for me, and I gave my heart to the Lord the next night. That was over 50 years ago, and the best decision I have ever made in my life.

CALL TO ACTION

I encourage you to reflect on your own life and consider if you have placed your trust in Jesus for your salvation. To grow in your faith, join a community of believers, read your bible and pray regularly.

ABOUT THE AUTHOR

CATHARINE LEONA JOY Minter Parks was born in Chatham, Ontario.

She spent her early childhood in the church, under a strict upbringing. But she soon wanted more. With an adventurous spirit, she would join her brother in sneaking out after bedtime.

They would go downtown to dances, plays, and movies. She wanted to enjoy the things her religious parents denied her. Catharine's love of words began in childhood. She would make up fake words and songs.

In 1983, she discovered her gift for songwriting. She recorded several songs, including "Proud to Be Canadian.

Mustard Seed Ministries published "A Glimpse of the Cross" on their site on January 25, 2007. Fate Magazine published "Cliffhanger" in November 2007. In June 2015, she published an e-book, "Heaven Sent Signs and Wonders." Supernatural events serve as the foundation.

On April 24, 2016, the publisher released Cat's Collection of Short Stories. In January 2016, she published 'Eye Rings.' It recounts her experience with eye floaters.

Other Books By Catharine LJ Parks

HEAVEN SENT SIGNS AND Wonders[1]
  Cat's Collection of Short Stories[2]
  Stepping into the Light[3]
  Eye Rings Revised[4]
  Are You Killing Your Obese Child With Food[5]
  Obese People Need Love Too[6]
  Obesity Strongholds: How to Overcome Them[7]
  I am a Keto Kid[8]

---

1. https://www.amazon.com/gp/product/B0108U7KCM

2.   https://www.amazon.com/gp/product/B01EPTMHJI

3.   https://www.amazon.com/gp/product/B07FRG5D4C

4.   https://www.amazon.com/gp/product/B01AOSEF08

5.   https://www.draft2digital.com/book/170302

6.   https://www.draft2digital.com/book/170603

7.   https://www.draft2digital.com/book/171057

8.   https://www.amazon.com/gp/product/B079ZCL2YS

Don't miss out!

Visit the website below and you can sign up to receive emails whenever Catharine LJ Parks publishes a new book. There's no charge and no obligation.

https://books2read.com/r/B-A-ABAD-DWOS

BOOKS 2 READ

Connecting independent readers to independent writers.

Also by Catharine LJ Parks

Obese People

Obesity Strongholds: How to Overcome Them

Standalone

For the Shattered Soul

The Ins and Outs of Gastric Bypass

Tips For Successful Dining Out

I am a Keto Kid

Why Remain Morbidly Obese

Ten Fads to Stay Clear of

Don't let Fear Win

Arguing With God

Heaven Sent Signs and Wonders

Watch for more at www.catharineljparks.com.

About the Author

Catharine Leona Joy Minter Parks was born in Chatham, Ontario. I am a Keto Kid was published in 2016; Obesity Strongholds and How to Overcome Them was published in May 2016; The Ins and Outs of Gastric Bypass, published July 27, 2017; Tips for Successful Dining Out, and Why Remain Morbidly Obese, was published in 2017.

Read more at www.catharineljparks.com.

About the Publisher